Lassie: A Dog's Life

The First Fifty Years

ACE COLLINS

CADER BOOKS

PENGUIN BOOKS

—To my dogs,
who have taught me a great deal about
love, loyalty, forgiveness, and honor.

—To Royal, Illinois, and Baylor University,
two places where I can always come home.

—And to Pal, the first of a great line.

PENGUIN BOOKS
Published by the Penguin Group
Penguin Books USA Inc., 375 Hudson Street, New York, New York 10014, U.S.A.
Penguin Books Ltd, 27 Wrights Lane, London W8 5TZ, England
Penguin Books Australia Ltd, Ringwood, Victoria, Australia
Penguin Books Canada Ltd, 10 Alcorn Avenue, Toronto, Ontario, Canada M4V 3B2
Penguin Books (N.Z.) Ltd, 182–190 Wairau Road, Auckland 10, New Zealand

Penguin Books Ltd, Registered Offices: Harmondsworth, Middlesex, England

First published in Penguin Books 1993

1 3 5 7 9 10 8 6 4 2

Produced by Cader Books
151 East 29 Street
New York, N.Y. 10016

ISBN 0 14 02.3183 8

Printed in the United States of America
Set in Adobe Garamond
Designed by Charles Kreloff with Steven M. Scott
Cover design by Michael Ian Kaye

Half title page: Pal and a happy offspring in a publicity shot for *Son of Lassie.*
Title page: The Lass.
Contents page: Any time is *Lassie* time.

Contents

The Lassie Lineage

Pal/Lassie I
The very first Lassie, this beautiful collie was the beginning of a long line of male dogs who continue to play the world's most famous female dog. Pal acted in all the MGM films and at age fourteen starred in the CBS television pilot, which aired as the first two episodes of *Lassie* in 1954. He died at the age of eighteen in 1958.

Lassie, Jr./Lassie II
The only Lassie whose name was really Lassie, this son of Pal became the first regular television dog, playing four years with Jeff and two more with Timmy. A cancerous tumor forced him to leave the show in 1959, and although he eventually recovered, he never returned to TV.

Spook
A son of Lassie, Jr., Spook is not considered an official Lassie; indeed he would never have appeared on the show at all if his more gifted sibling had not fallen ill. For just over a half year—in the spring of 1960 and again in the fall—he struggled through the starring role, terrified of actors, sets, and lights. In an odd twist, it is substitute Spook who appears in the opening credits of the Timmy-era show walking with Jon Provost.

Baby/Lassie III
Starting work in 1960, finishing out the Timmy years of the series, and continuing on for the first two seasons of the Ranger era, Baby starred on *Lassie* for six years. His career was cut short when he, like his father, developed cancer, and he died in 1966 at the age of eight, the only Lassie who did not live at least seventeen years.

Mire/Lassie IV

Mire played Lassie for five years during the Ranger shows, negotiating the switch in 1968 from single- to double-ranger format. His selection as the new Lassie was a difficult one, for both he and his brother Muck were fine candidates; Muck eventually became Mire's stand-in. Lassie IV, Mire, lived to be nineteen.

Hey Hey/Lassie V

The last of the television Lassies, Hey Hey was the featured dog in the syndicated version of the show. After his TV career ended in 1974 he continued to work for many years, playing live shows across the country. He died at eighteen.

Boy/Lassie VI

The son of Hey Hey, Boy brought Lassie back to the big screen with *The Magic of Lassie* in 1978. He also danced on stage with the Rockettes at Radio City Music Hall. He died in 1989, just a few years after his father.

The Old Man/Lassie VII

Lassie VII, son of Boy and just a young dog when Rudd Weatherwax died, became the last Lassie the famed master trained. His education was taken over by Rudd's son Robert, and later he starred in *The New Lassie*, the syndicated show that ran in the late eighties and early nineties.

Howard/Lassie VIII

The largest Lassie yet, Howard made his debut at the 1993 Tournament of Roses Parade and has done numerous appearances since then. Robert Weatherwax is now training Howard, the great-great-great-great-great-grandson of Pal, to star in the next *Lassie* film.

Foreword

bout two years ago I took my sable-and-white collie for one of her weekly visits to a local nursing home. These treks offered Lady, a licensed therapy dog, a chance to meet people, give some senior dog lovers an opportunity for hands-on encounters, and, I hoped, provide some canine sunshine to an often dark world.

On this occasion the head nurse asked me to stop by a room where the door had always been closed, one I had never before visited. With Nurse Hafer leading us, Lady entered, glanced up at an elderly woman in a wheelchair, and, upon receiving my hand signal, crossed the room and laid her head in the woman's lap. Slowly, as if waking, Mrs. Burton studied the dog before allowing her long thin fingers to stroke Lady's head. After a few minutes of this, she looked up at me and observed, "She looks like Lassie."

In my mind Lady bore only a passing resemblance to the famous collie. She was the proper color and the right size, but she didn't have a full white collar or that famous Lassie blaze down her face. Still, long ago I had come to expect people's first words upon seeing Lady to be "Look, it's a Lassie!"

As Mrs. Burton petted Lady she spoke to me about taking her children to see Lassie movies back in the forties. She talked about the films' plots and stars, and she marveled over the things Lassie had been able to do. She then mentioned that she and her grandchildren had spent many Sunday nights in front of the television watching Jeff and Lassie, then Timmy and Lassie, and finally Ranger Stuart and Lassie. As she spoke in a halting whisper, she also laughed: Lassie, she explained, had meant a great deal to three generations of her family.

After about five minutes it was time for Lady and me to move on to another room, so I said good-bye, Lady kissed Mrs. Burton on the cheek, and we walked out with the nurse. In the hallway I noticed tears in Nurse Hafer's blue eyes.

"What's wrong?" I asked.

"Mrs. Burton hasn't spoken in nearly two years," she said quietly. "She had a severe stroke and no one ever thought she would talk again. Your dog has just performed a miracle."

As we walked into the next room and Lady repeated her bit of Wednesday-morning magic for another resident, I realized that Lady had not created the miracle, Lassie had. Lassie had left impressions so deep that they could temporarily heal an old woman's short-circuited mind; Lassie had so touched her heart that things she had long forgotten came back to her. In Mrs. Burton's mind it was Lassie whom she held in her hands on that day, and it was Lassie who had awakened her spirit. For that instant, in that room, Lassie had come home.

Lassie, the bedtime story.

So for good reason do we celebrate the fiftieth anniversary of one of the world's greatest and best-known personalities. After all, she is a superstar. Lassie's name has been featured above those of Elizabeth Taylor, Roddy McDowall, June Lockhart, Mickey Rooney, Janet Leigh, and James Stewart. For a time she was one of MGM's biggest money-makers, and she was one of the few figures who successfully made the switch from movies to radio in the forties and then to television in the fifties.

Lassie's television show ran for more than twenty years, negotiated six different formats, survived five supporting-cast changes, and remained near the top of the Nielsen ratings for almost its entire run. Lassie has graced nine *TV Guide* covers and has been featured in *Life, Saturday Evening Post,* and countless other regional, national, and international periodicals.

Lassie is a star with amazing resilience. In the late seventies, after her television show was canceled, she went back to movies, working with some of the top names in the business. She even danced on the stage of Radio City Music Hall. A survivor of Hollywood's golden era, she even has her own star in the "Walk of Fame."

With the possible exception of Bob Hope, no other star has successfully made as many entertainment transitions as Lassie. And yet after five decades in the business, she seems to have no enemies—there have been no backbiting stories concerning how she clawed her way to the top, and no scandals have been associated with her name. Of course there is the fact that *she* was actually a *he,* but the eight generations of male dogs who have filled Lassie's prints have combined to create one of film and video's most lasting images. Also like Bob Hope, Lassie's origins were English, but it is

This Lassie View-master is one of the most favored of the great collie's collectibles.

in the United States that the dog has been so embraced.

In the thirties and forties, Hollywood stars were given nick-names that drew attention to their best qualities. Jean Harlow was "the Platinum Blonde," John Barrymore was "the Great Profile," Lauren Bacall was "the Look," and an MGM press agent dubbed Lassie "the Bark." Undoubtedly that handle is one of the most appropriate ever given to a film actor.

Celebrating her show-business golden anniversary, Lassie is not only an American institution but one of the best-known and most-loved animals in the world. The story of Lassie, who was once described as "Greer Garson in furs," reads like Cinderella without the wicked stepmother.

Lassie began life as a simple sentimental dog story written by a man who would die in World War II. Eric Knight's novel, *Lassie Come-Home*, has touched generation after generation. A common man with common dreams, Knight thus became the father of one of the world's most beloved figures. So it seems appropriate that his moving tale about a collie of the highest breeding would become the springboard to superstardom not for a show dog but for an unwanted, unregistered dog known as Pal.

Over the course of fifty years, those who have written Lassie's roles have given the award-winning actor little to say. While others, including a certain well-known television horse and a film-star mule, were handed pages of dialogue, the collie was forced to communicate with energy, charm, expression, action, and a simple "woof." In the long history of film, never has an actor used one word to convey so many emotions in so many different situations. Even more amazing, for more than fifty years we have believed that she understood everything said to her—that she could communicate pain, anger, love, and happiness, her very heart and soul, with a simple woof and those big brown eyes.

How big a star would Gary Cooper, Bette Davis, or Humphrey Bogart have been if their writers had allowed them to use only one word? Could they have expressed so many emotions and so much depth limited to just one syllable? Would we have fallen in love with them the way we fell in love with Lassie? Could they have so touched a woman's memory as to create a miracle?

Just a few weeks ago I took my Lady to visit an elementary school. As I walked into a second-grade classroom, twenty children cried out all at once, "It's Lassie!" Five decades after the MGM movie and almost twenty years since the television show ran on CBS, a group of children, most without cable television, still knew that a sable-and-white collie was Lassie.

Fifty years of making us laugh and cry, fifty years as a real "bone-ified" star, fifty years of heroic images—these combine for more than just another dog story. Lassie's life is clearly something to remember and celebrate, for in one way or another she has changed the world. Unlike so many others who have walked away never to return, Lassie has never failed to come home. But, of course, Lassie's home has always been in our hearts.

The Men Behind the Dog:
How the Lassie Legend Grew

LASSIE-METRO GOLDWYN MAYER

*N*oble, brave, and smart, Lassie has established herself over the last fifty years as one of the world's most beloved heroines. The dog that actually portrayed Lassie, however, was not a female at all but a male. So it seems only appropriate that a male dog playing a female character would have two fathers. One, Eric Knight, created the captivating story of Lassie, and the other, Rudd Weatherwax, nurtured and trained the real-life dog who made the character into a star. But before either of these two "fathers" had any notion of Lassie and what Lassie would become, each owned a very special collie dog, and that is where the tale of Lassie truly begins.

Lassie was first conceived in the heart and the mind of Eric Knight, a scholar, movie critic, playwright, and author who would eventually become an American war hero and die at the age of forty-five in World War II. In his short life Knight rose from poverty to fame, from an unknown lad who moved to America from England at the age of eleven to a distinguished author working with America's revered filmmaker Frank Capra. Still, Knight's greatest aspiration was not fame or fortune—rather, he had an overwhelming desire to write the great American novel. Yet it was his simple and sentimental dog story, *Lassie Come-Home*, that would catapult him to fame. He was in his own way a genius, a master of vivid phrases and a gifted storyteller, but he was also a humble man who sensed that his life's most cherished moments could be found not on the bustling streets of Hollywood but in the gentler moments spent on a Pennsylvania farm. And on that farm in Bucks County, Pennsylvania, Knight's other passion besides writing found a home, for there he and his wife, Jere, raised collies.

As important as their dogs were to Eric and Jere, in the fall of 1934 the couple was forced to sell their kennel and all of their collies so that they could move to Hollywood, where Eric was to be employed as a story consultant at Fox Film Corporation. They took only a little fox terrier with them, but within days of their arrival in California the dog was killed. As Jere explained, "From that instant I hated Hollywood and everything there.

"Then Christmas came along," Jere recalled, "and Eric came home with a little collie puppy tucked in the pocket of his tweed

Previous page: Pal, the first Lassie and the greatest movie dog who ever lived.

French for Dogs

Eric Knight rarely traveled without his faithful collie companion, Toots, the inspiration for *Lassie Come-Home*. She was treated more like a child than a dog, and she thrived on this special care. Knight worked with her daily to develop a long list of tricks that were well known to those who visited his Pennsylvania farm.

Once on an automobile trip to Canada to promote one of his novels, Knight decided to show a gathering of his northern neighbors just how smart his American dog was. He asked the dog to sit, lie down, roll over, speak, shake, and fetch. Toots did them all flawlessly, and those in attendance applauded these "normal" dog tricks.

Smiling, Knight then bragged that the dog understood not only English but Canada's second language, French. He then explained that he didn't speak French but that his wife did, and so with Jere Knight giving the commands, Toots once again performed perfectly. Again the crowd was amazed. Everyone agreed that Toots was something very special indeed, a bilingual canine. Taking it a step further, Knight then had Toots go through a routine of stunts in German. Trilingual!

Unknown to the adoring crowd, Toots was trained to respond to hand rather than voice signals. During each command she hadn't listened to the words at all but had looked to Knight for a certain hand motion. The signals were so understated that no one ever caught on.

Eric Knight with his beloved collie Toots, the inspiration for Lassie Come-Home.

jacket. From the first day both of us gave a lot of attention to that dog, and our bond with Toots was tremendously close. Yet, as much time as we both spent with her, she was definitely Eric's dog."

When Eric Knight wasn't writing, he was spending time training Toots. His positive approach with animals included large doses of love and rewards. He gently asked the new puppy to do something and then praised her mightily when she did. The best pupil he had ever had, Toots constantly amazed Eric with her intelligence and potential.

Eric Knight illustrated his original short story with several of his own drawings. This offering shows Lassie watching a traveling salesman's dog perform.

"Eric trained her with both verbal commands and hand signals," Jere remembered, "and she could do almost anything he asked. Toots had the most remarkable vocabulary, and he enjoyed showing her off. She was his constant shadow and he somehow understood every twitch of her nostrils. He knew her every look, and she rarely took her eyes off him."

A gift of love for his mourning wife, Toots would become Eric Knight's best friend. The robust, good-looking, redheaded man and

the beautiful, well-groomed black dog with sable and white mark-ings—known as a tricolor to collie fanciers—were inseparable. They rode all around Los Angeles together and took long walks in the late evenings. Toots was always by Knight's side even as he la-bored over his stories and plays. She was like no dog he had ever known, and yet she was the very dog for which he had longed since his childhood in Yorkshire, England, the collie he never had.

Each evening she would wait by the stone wall in front of their rural home for her master to come home. She would watch the road, her eyes following each movement. When he would fi-nally arrive, Toots would leap for joy, race up to his side, and the two of them would walk slowly up to the house. Knight's coming home was the most important thing in her life.

In the early winter of 1938, Knight left for England to report on five distressed industrial areas for the *Saturday Evening Post.* While there he was deeply struck by the poverty of his native York-shire. The area's prized collies meant almost as much to the people as their families, but in order to pay for food, clothing, and fuel, many Yorkshire dog owners were being forced to sell the animals that had been their workers, companions, and beloved pets.

This distressing sight, coupled with the image of Toots racing to meet him as he strolled through the gate, became the inspira-tion for Knight's short story "Lassie Come-Home." Drawing on the rich memories of his youth, Knight wove a heartfelt tale of a family forced by poverty to sell their extraordinary collie to a rich man, who spirits the dog off to Scotland. Desolate at the separa-tion from her family, the dog escapes and travels alone across Scot-land and England, enduring terrible hardships as she struggles and finally successfully returns home. The story was moving, but Knight's wife and daughters protested that he was being too cruel by putting this fictional dog through so much. Still Knight recog-nized just how much Toots would go through to be with him, and he knew that no obstacle could stand between his dog and her master. He had also felt the pain of the people of Yorkshire at the loss of their dogs, and he used all these things to write a story more about love and loyalty than about just a dog and an owner.

In December 1938 the *Saturday Evening Post* printed the short story. Within a few weeks a small Bible and children's book publisher in Philadelphia, the John C. Winston Company, asked Knight to expand "Lassie Come-Home" into a novel. It took him only a few weeks to finish the work, which he dedicated "To Dr. Harry Jarrett, a man who knows dogs."

The veterinarian whom Eric Knight admired so is largely credited with introducing and popularizing the collie breed in the United States. Jarrett, the author's best friend, was also the only individual with whom Knight would leave Toots when the family was away from the farm on business and could not bring the collie along. Certainly it is appropriate that Jarrett, a man with such a deep love for the collie breed, was in a small way immortalized in this book about what would become the world's most famous dog.

Lassie Come-Home was released in May 1940 and became an immediate best-seller. "This is more than a good dog-story," reviewer Lamberton Becker wrote. "It may well be found, a long time hence, to be among the dog-stories that do not go out of print." Winston released five printings during the first six months of publication. Toots, the book's inspiration, had become a national hero, and yet she was oblivious to her new fame. She only cared that her master, with a smile on his face, met her at the gate each evening.

About the time Eric Knight was on triumphant book tours for *Lassie Come-Home*, Lassie's other "father," dog trainer Rudd Weatherwax, was working away in Hollywood under a veil of frustrated obscurity. After almost two decades in the motion-picture business, Rudd was still trying to establish himself as a top-flight trainer worthy of a regular studio salary—and this despite the fact that he was training Asta, the terrier from the *Thin Man* series, and the mutt Daisy from the *Blondie* series, two of the biggest stars in dog business. Times were so tough that to supplement their meager studio incomes, Rudd and his brothers had pooled their resources and opened a dog-training center to help solve the problems of non-Hollywood dogs. While he might have been able to train Asta to help detective Nick Charles solve mysteries, and while he could

Lassie's Famous Stablemates

*L*ong before Rudd worked with his famous collie, Pal, he had trained some of the most prominent dogs in film history. He began his training career as a teenager with his own pet, a small mutt named Wriggles, who made scores of appearances in silent movies. Then, in the early thirties, Rudd trained a little dog called Corky for a film called *Peck's Bad Boy.* The dog and the film's juvenile star, Jackie Cooper, worked so well together that many believed Corky must have actually belonged to Jackie.

Also during the thirties, two of Rudd's pupils made lasting impressions in a duo of long-running movie series. In the *Thin Man* movies, the first of which was released in 1934, Rudd worked with Asta and later with Asta, Jr., the terriers who stole scene after scene from Myrna Loy and William Powell. And in the *Blondie* series, which started a few years later, Rudd trained Daisy and all of her pups.

In addition, the trainer worked with the dog in *Old Yeller,* a huge hound who rescues his young master from a ravening beast and eventually pays with his life. Weatherwax also trained the dogs that appeared in the 3-D John Wayne spectacular *Hondo* from 1953, and its 1971 sequel, *Big Jake.* Pal's son and grandson respectively, the two collies who played these parts were also the personal pets of Robert, Rudd's son.

Long before Lassie ever entered the picture, Rudd Weatherwax had made a name for himself in the dog business by training the terriers who played Asta in the Thin Man *movies.*

make Daisy look smarter than Dagwood, Rudd was paying a large part of his bills by teaching regular people's dogs how to heel.

Rudd, the other human element needed to bring the fictional character of Lassie to life, was the son of an Arizona rancher who had once ridden with Buffalo Bill. Rudd's pioneer stock was deeply rooted by the generations of Weatherwaxes who had helped shape the western frontier. As a boy, Rudd with his collie dog worked herds of sheep and goats on the wide open range. When he was a teenager he left high school and began training his own animals for the struggling motion-picture industry. In the golden age of Hollywood he and his brothers opened a business devoted to preparing dogs for the movies. Time passed and he earned more and more respect from his peers, but he was forever eyeing the thousands of canines he handled, hoping to find the next dog star—a canine with all the box-office capabilities of Rin Tin Tin.

Like Eric Knight, Rudd Weatherwax was a charismatic man who never lacked for company. While he searched for the perfect German shepherd, he worked on hundreds of sets, where he made friends with some of the greatest stars in the business. Humphrey Bogart and Gary Cooper always had time to share a drink and swap stories with the talented and colorful Rudd. But even though his circle of friends included the Who's Who of film, by the late thirties Rudd wasn't doing much more than just paying the bills. So he could never have dreamed that his name would soon be famous, forever linked to one of the biggest stars of all time. As a matter of fact, he was working so hard to make ends meet that he scarcely had time to dream at all.

But the dog that would change Rudd's life—and Hollywood's—was barking just around the corner. Their first meeting wasn't particularly auspicious. As Rudd's son Robert explained, "Howard Peck, a famous Hollywood animal trainer, had been hired by a man to stop an eight-month-old collie puppy named Pal from chasing motorcycles and barking all the time. When Howard couldn't get him to quit, he brought the dog to my father. Well, Dad worked with the dog for a while, and after a time he got the barking under control, but he couldn't get him to stop chasing

The start of it all: Pal and his trainer, Rudd Weatherwax, together in 1942.

motorcycles—as a matter of fact, the dog did that until the day he died. Howard told Dad, 'Well, if it's going to chase motorcycles the owner doesn't want it, and neither do I. Instead of taking payment on the animal, you can keep it.'

"In reality Dad couldn't keep the collie because he was a trainer and employed by the studios, and there was just no work for collies in motion pictures," Robert continued. "He knew that Pal was smart, and he loved the way the dog responded to basic training, but this was a business and he couldn't just let him stay without getting something from him. So he farmed the dog out to an actor friend of his. Dad told him, 'You can keep him, and if I ever need him, I'll get him back.'"

Rudd figured he would never see Pal again. The dog, now completely free to roam on a large ranch filled with rabbits, briars, and thickets, probably never thought he would see the trainer, a bath, or a brush again. Pal soon forgot his more cultured training and became a happy, carefree fleabag.

But a few months later, his mind still set on discovering the next Rin Tin Tin, Rudd was wandering about the MGM lot and overheard someone talking about a new property that the company had just purchased. "Can you believe that they paid $10,000 for a dog story?" one man incredulously asked another. Rudd listened intently as the two men shared a laugh, and then, after catching the name of the book, he dashed across the lot. He was familiar with the story line of Eric Knight's *Lassie Come-Home*, and he knew its potential as a movie. When he considered what would be needed from the animal that would play the lead, it dawned on him that he might have given away the one dog that could meet the demands of the part.

Running to the nearest phone, Rudd called the actor who now had Pal and asked him for the dog back. Unfortunately the new owner had grown to like the spunky, active collie and balked until Rudd offered him ten dollars. A few hours later, checkbook in hand, the dog trainer purchased the now completely unkempt and bedraggled collie. Pal looked no more like the lead for *Lassie Come-Home* than Rudd did Bette Davis, yet the trainer was convinced he could bring the dog into shape.

Just as David O. Selznick searched the nation for an unknown to play Scarlett in *Gone with the Wind*, MGM executives ordered a national search to find just the right dog to play Lassie. Talent scouts raced from city to city and dog show to dog show looking at every show-quality champion female collie that they could find. Over 1,500 dogs were photographed, checked, and rechecked, and Pal was one of them. At Pal's audition the experts told Rudd that his dog's "eyes were too big, his coat was in miserable shape, his head was too flat," Weatherwax's son Robert recalled. "And that ugly white blaze running down the dog's forehead made him look like anything but a prize-winning dog. He might be smart, he might be able to do more than fifty tricks, but that was not enough. Who would believe a collie like this one was the famous Lassie from the book? Besides," Robert described the judges pointing out, "he is a male."

Lassie traveled the world via the pages of Dell comics, beginning in 1949 and running for twenty years.

As he left the audition, Rudd felt that the judges had sold Pal short. If they had seen him work, he knew, their minds would have been changed. So even as the search went on, he took Pal back home, formulated a special diet, groomed him daily, and soon had the once ragged coat in top shape. Through his own positive, reward-focused training system he also continued to add to the canine's repertoire of stunts and tricks. Rudd was sure he would get a second chance, and so when he felt Pal was at his peak he took him back to the studio for another look.

The transformation from ragged beast to beauty was impressive, but while the powers at MGM couldn't believe that this was the same dog they had viewed earlier, he still wasn't deemed good enough. Instead they were going to go with a show-winning female. Nevertheless, they liked Rudd's work, so they hired him to train their new "star." Pal, now over a year old, was also hired as the stunt dog. Things stood that way for almost six weeks before the paw of fate moved again.

Lassie Come Home (the studio had now dropped the dash from between the *Come* and the *Home*) was being shot as a B movie, just another black-and-white film. MGM saw the movie as an action adventure film stocked with a dog, a host of character actors and contract players, plus a couple of unknown kids with British accents named Roddy McDowall and Elizabeth Taylor. This was not a big-budget offering—the studio just wanted something that the kids would like and that would make a few dollars. So when shortcuts could be taken, they were.

A few weeks into filming, the San Joaquin River in central California flooded, an event that offered a wonderful opportunity to capture some great footage without spending any money on special effects. Grabbing color cameras, the only type available that day, the crew, the cast, and the dogs headed north for a location shoot. It took hours to get everything set. Then, with the cameras in place, all eyes fell on the slightly spoiled and very nervous show dog. The script called for Lassie to jump into a raging river, swim to the other side, and finally pull herself out of the stream. But again and again the female star refused her owner's pleas to get into the water. Panic gripped the location and a conference was called.

Pal was always good, so Santa always remembered him on Christmas.

After some heated discussions between director and crew, Rudd Weatherwax stepped in and pointed out that all wet dogs look pretty much alike from a distance. His own collie was there on the set, and Pal could and would, Rudd insisted, swim the stream. With the clock ticking and Mr. Mayer back at the studio keeping track of expenditures, the crew had little choice but to go with Rudd and the furry motorcycle chaser. About an hour later, after Rudd had prepped the dog, Pal jumped into the flooded San Joaquin.

By all accounts it was an extremely nervous crew that watched Rudd and Pal go to work that day, and with good reason. The water was unpredictable, the dog was a complete mystery to everyone but the trainer, and the daylight was passing quickly. Everyone expected that several takes would be required to get this shot right, but they also realized they just didn't have that much

Lassie the Female Impersonator

One of the most urgent Lassie questions concerns why only male dogs have played Lassie. In fact the studio originally hired a female for the lead in *Lassie Come Home*. What MGM didn't know was that female collies lose a large part of their coats each time they go into heat. Mature females go into heat twice a year, and this can destroy the dog's appearance for as much as a third of the year. As shooting began, the female chosen for the lead was beginning to lose her coat, and a collie out of coat is anything but a beautiful animal. But ultimately she was unwilling to deal with the requirements of the part—swimming a raging river was beyond the pale for this finely bred show dog. After the versatile Pal stepped into the part and became a star, using a female was out of the question.

Rudd Weatherwax himself believed that female dogs were generally smarter and easier to work with than males. But from the first he argued against using a female. Male collies also shed their coats, he knew, but only once a year, so it would be far easier to shoot around a male's loss of coat. In addition, Weatherwax realized that a larger collie would appear much more impressive. The male's greater size would make Lassie look heroic, which is how the audience needed to perceive her.

Roddy McDowall and Pal check out Eric Knight's novel to make sure the scriptwriters were following the original story line.

time. What they needed was a miracle.

"The script read, 'Lassie jumps in the river, swims across the stream and comes out exhausted,'" Robert Weatherwax explained. "Well, Dad designed a shot where Pal swims across the stream, comes out, does not shake (because a tired dog would not shake water off), and lies down. Then he attempts to crawl while lying on his side, and finally, appearing completely exhausted, lies motionless. This was a five-stage shot."

The film's director, Fred Wilcox, watched in amazement as Pal launched himself into the water and without protest swam through the swirling rapids. Just as he had been coached, Pal didn't even shake the water from his coat before lying down and pretending to be almost dead from exhaustion. He lay there for over a minute waiting for his trainer's next command, all the while not moving as much as the tip of his tail. A five-stage shot had been completed, perfectly, in one take and on the first try.

"Cut," the director cried out, and as he did the crew broke into applause. Even as the ovation built, Pal remained motionless. Only when Rudd approached him and shouted "Good boy!" did he bounce up and shake the water from his coat.

Running up to Rudd, director Wilcox blurted out, "That dog that jumped into the river may have been Pal, but it was Lassie who crawled out. Your dog is my star, I don't care what anyone says!" Wilcox was true to his word. The first collie was immediately fired, and Pal won the leading role. Just as if it had been scripted, a star was born.

Back at the studio, Mayer was so impressed with the rushes that he ordered *Lassie Come Home* to be produced as an A movie. This meant great publicity, full advertising support, and Technicolor. Pal's swim had changed everything. Within days, filming was kicked into high gear and the public was told that a magical movie was being made on the MGM lot.

A few months later Eric Knight, in Hollywood again and working with director Frank Capra, visited the set to watch his best-selling book come to life. As he observed from just off camera, his heart was immediately captured by the film's star. Pal wasn't a

It Doesn't Matter if You're Black or White

Thanks to Pal and the seven generations of descendants that have followed him, Lassie will forever be seen as a sable-and-white collie with a white blaze running from between the eyes down to the powder puff at the nose, a full white collar of fur around the neck, and four white feet. But the fact is that Eric Knight never intended for his Lassie to be a sable-and-white dog.

In Knight's famous book, Lassie is described as a tricolor, a dog that is principally black with white and sable highlights, or markings, on the face and tail. The jacket of *Lassie Come-Home* clearly presents Lassie as a "tri." But Pal changed all that.

In addition to the fact that he was the "wrong" color, Pal's blaze was also a point of concern for collie fanciers, for the mark was looked upon with great disdain by breeders. For generations there had been attempts to breed it out, and by the forties this had been largely successful. So when millions of children saw the film *Lassie Come Home* and requested a collie of their own, breeders had to scramble to breed the blaze back into their stock.

Besides sables and tris, there are also white and blue-merle collies. The whites have either a tricolor or sable head, while the blues are shaded much like an Australian sheepdog. Most people do not know that all collies carry a gene for short hair and that some end up with "smooth" coats, as short fur is called—about the same length as the fur of a common German shepherd. Smooth-coat collies also come in all four colors.

Rudd Weatherwax was assisted throughout the earlier years of his career by Frank Inn, who later trained another famous movie dog, Benji.

tricolor collie like Toots, and he definitely wasn't a show dog like the character in his book, but he was magnificent in a way that only a person who knew dogs could truly realize—intelligent, with so much heart, and so devoted to the man who gently urged him on.

"Everything about him is right," Knight informed Fred Wilcox. Seeing the dog work, having the animal's broad head under his hand, looking into his large, almond-shaped eyes, tracing the blaze that ran up Pal's forehead, the author knew he had found a soul mate. Here was a dog who could bring Knight's words and dreams alive, and this Lassie had been graced with an owner who loved him as much as the book's

Joe Carraclough, the boy who had owned Lassie only to be forced to sell her. There was no doubt that Pal would brave the elements and travel miles to get home to Rudd Weatherwax just as the book's Lassie had traveled the length of England to find Joe.

For Knight and Weatherwax, *Lassie Come Home* was a movie, a job, and a moment in life when both of them were able to participate in something magical that they really loved. At that time they wouldn't have asked for anything more. Yet something had been set in motion that was beyond their control. In the midst of a world war, a legend was being created from one man's novel and another's belief in a dog no one really wanted. That legend would grow bigger than either of the men, outlive them both, and make Lassie an American icon.

A Star Is Born:
The Triumph of
Lassie Come Home

As Pal crossed that mighty river from one bank to the other, he was elevated from obscurity to everlasting fame. To get there, all the dog had to do was act, and as those initial rushes clearly proved, he was a natural and he loved to work. As Rudd Weatherwax would say time and time again, "He was a ham."

With Weatherwax's skilled preparation and the talented collie's abilities and enthusiasm, Pal simply didn't need the multiple takes or the extensive training and retraining that most animal and human actors required. He was always ready for action. He never hesitated, never balked, always responded in the way that had been fashioned for him, and when something new arose, he handled it far better than most of the crew. He didn't even require stunt doubles as he hurdled walls, faked fights, pulled humans from swirling rapids, and spoke on cue. The truth may have been lost on most of those who worked around this mass of sable-and-white fur, but there could be no doubt that Weatherwax's almost two decades in the film industry had a great deal to do with making Pal and director Fred Wilcox look like geniuses. If the dog appeared brilliant, it was because there was an even more brilliant man behind him urging him every step of the way.

Still, even though he now loved and admired Pal as he had no other dog, Rudd Weatherwax kept telling himself that this was just another job, a one-shot deal. Movies starring dogs had dried up even before talking pictures had become the Hollywood staple, and industry wisdom said that they would never start again. Pal wasn't even receiving star treatment. He and the trainer rode in baggage cars to location shots, ate beef stew out of cans, and didn't have a dressing room. Pal was a darn good dog, but that was all. So it seemed likely to Rudd that making good money and being on a weekly payroll would end as quickly as it had begun.

"Lassie is not the first great dog star," Rudd told everyone. "The great canine stars of Hollywood, going back to the very beginning, were German shepherds like Rin Tin Tin, Flash, and the greatest of them all, Strongheart. Lassie breaks the mold because he is a different breed. He probably is only to be a one-shot star." Strongheart had been a muscled package of black-and-silver energy

Previous page: A handsome dog indeed, but most agreed that Betty Grable looked a lot better on a bearskin rug than the studio's most famous canine.

who supplied more action in a minute than most cowboy pictures did in an hour. In the classic days of silent movies he was Hollywood's most dramatic canine star, and now he was Weatherwax's prototype of the great dog.

When Donald Crisp joined the cast of *Lassie Come Home,* he had expected nothing more than the paycheck and a chance to wrap his wonderful accent around some well-written dialogue. Yet from the moment he saw Pal it was love at first sight. Although he couldn't initially put his finger on it, there was something about this collie that appealed to him tremendously. As the days of filming turned into weeks, Crisp and Pal became fast friends. Crisp spent hours getting to know the collie, observing his movement, his manner, and his actions. He studied the way the dog solved problems, learned stunts, and sensed what was expected of him. He marveled at how eager Pal was to hear the word "Action." Fi-

Nigel Bruce took leave of his most famous role, that of Dr. Watson in the Sherlock Holmes movies, to play Liz Taylor's grandfather in the initial Lassie movie. Bruce would recreate the role in Son of Lassie.

nally, almost halfway through filming, Crisp figured it out. He knew why Pal had gotten to him the moment they had met. He pulled Weatherwax to one side.

"Your dog reminds me of Strongheart," Crisp said with admiration. And the actor would know, for as it turned out Rudd's hero, Strongheart, had belonged to Crisp's wife. "When he got sick and died at the age of fourteen, I held him in my arms as he breathed his last. I visit his grave in my backyard still, and your Pal is so much like him."

Pal's Parents

The identity of Pal's true parents was debated for many years, Rudd Weatherwax and MGM both claiming that the dog's birth records were lost. Some reports even went so far as to question whether Pal was a purebred dog. In truth, Pal's family tree can be traced back to the nineteenth century, to England's first great collie, Old Cockie.

While Pal was never registered, he was the product of one of the West Coast's best-known collie kennels, Cherry Osborne's Glamis Kennels of North Hollywood. Osborne's dogs had won a host of championships and her kennels were the base of some of the era's best-bred dogs. In an effort to continuously improve her stock, she would bring in for stud such collie legends as Silver Ho's Shining Arrow. But Pal, because he had a large blaze down his nose and big eyes, was not judged an improvement, so he was sold as a pet-quality dog.

Pal's parents were both North Hollywood blue bloods, Red Brucie of Glamis and Bright Bauble of Glamis. Through kennel records and American Kennel Club registration of his litter, Pal's birth date has been fixed as June 4, 1940. Rudd Weatherwax was given no blue slip (the AKC registration form) when the dog was left in his care, and because his business was dog training and not breeding or showing, he never sought to obtain one. Hence, Pal was never registered, a fact of no concern to Weatherwax. (Coincidentally, exactly one year after Pal's birth, on June 4, 1941, Rudd's youngest son and the current Lassie trainer, Robert Weatherwax, was born in Los Angeles; like Pal, he also came without a blue slip.)

Throughout the remainder of the shoot, Crisp and Pal went for daily walks in the morning, often accompanied by Rudd. In the afternoons as they waited for camera setups, the actor would bring a ball or stick and play with Pal. It was as if Pal had found a mentor, an old man to show him the ropes. Then, one day, without any explanation, Crisp refused even to acknowledge the dog's presence. Pal was destroyed. This treatment went on day after day, and the dog, almost panicked that his good friend ignored him, tried to break this evil spell with whines, yelps, tugs and moans. Finally, in a last desperate attempt, Pal approached Crisp as he sat in a familiar spot on the family home set. Desperate for the old actor's approval, Pal waited until Rudd signaled that it was all right, then, in a most hesitant manner, the animal gingerly approached Crisp, stuck his muzzle under his hand, and for several moments begged to be noticed. Just after the director yelled "Cut," Crisp smiled and hugged his canine friend.

The crew, who had been in on the reason behind Crisp's behavior, went wild. The cagey old veteran had used Pal's affection to help create a scene in which it appeared that Lassie longed desperately for Crisp's character's approval. Crisp had employed this same method with Strongheart many years before, and it had worked then too. But like the German shepherd before him, poor Pal didn't know it was a scene—he had been playing it for real. While the crew clapped and whistled, Pal must have thought they were celebrating that he had somehow won back his old friend.

"Lassie is sensitive," director Wilcox explained during the film's first press tour, "and he also likes to work." Laughing, he added, "It didn't take him very long to figure out that he was the star, and he grew to love the attention. One of the things that

One of Pal's favorite costars, Donald Crisp, first developed a great love and admiration for Pal while working on Lassie Come Home. Crisp was reunited with the dog a few years later on both Challenge to Lassie and Hills of Home.

made our job so easy is that he would do almost anything to get that attention."

This was Wilcox's first directing assignment—it had been tossed his way simply because MGM didn't want to waste one of their more renowned directors on a dog movie—so the ease with which he was able to film each scene was very important. Just like the dog's career, Wilcox's whole future in Hollywood would be based on the footage he assembled for *Lassie Come Home.*

"In a scene where Lassie dug his way under a fence, we just locked him in and called him," the director told the media. "He began digging and in no time he was out." Wilcox discovered that Lassie was far easier to direct than most human stars. The dog's ego didn't get in the way of camera angles or lines of dialogue. Pal couldn't conceive that anything was impossible or too hard, and he loved to work. Besides, Clark Gable and Katharine Hepburn seemed to regard a pat on the head as an inadequate reward.

Pawtographed Pictures

At the height of his MGM popularity, Pal was asked for literally thousands of autographs each week. As smart as he was, he couldn't write, and he certainly didn't like to have his foot dipped in ink hundreds of times a day. So to enable Pal to personally fulfill his many autograph requests, Rudd Weatherwax made a plaster cast of the dog's foot, which was turned into an ink stamp. With several of these in hand, he set about stamping thousands of pictures of the famous dog. They proved to be immensely popular, so much so that Rudd made hundreds more stamps and turned the job over to MGM personnel.

Over the course of the next five decades, hundreds of thousands of "pawtographed" photos were produced in this manner. As the years passed and the Lassie mantle was handed down from son to son, new publicity photos were constantly introduced. Yet, in tribute to the original dog, Pal's stamp was used throughout the movie and television run, and is still in use today.

"Let's shake on it," Pal *seems to be saying as a young starlet comes by to watch him sign his* MGM *contract.*

When *Lassie Come Home* was previewed by the MGM executives behind the lot walls in 1943, crusty Louis B. Mayer cried. So moved was he by what he saw that he ordered more scenes to be filmed to enhance what he called "this wonderful motion picture." He also cranked up his publicity department another notch— MGM unleashed hundreds of stills of Pal on the set, off the set, eating, walking, sitting, sleeping, and playing. One of these shots even showed Pal—always referred to as Lassie in the releases— placing his paw print on an MGM contract while a bathing-suit clad starlet looked on.

Learning the Murderous Snarl

Revered heroine and American celebrity, Lassie—in the form of Pal—was invited in the late forties to sit for a painting by Norman Rockwell. The artist was planning a work called *Murder Mystery*, a parody of English mystery stories that would show a murdered man surrounded by friends and relatives, one of whom was responsible for his death. Rockwell had arranged to have major film stars pose for the cast of characters in his picture, among them Ethel Barrymore and Lassie.

For Lassie's role in the painting, which was eventually rejected by the *Saturday Evening Post* because the staff didn't understand it, Rockwell wanted the dog to snarl. But Pal was incapable of producing a ferocious look and instead just looked happily back at the painter. Rudd, as it turned out, had never taught Pal how to snarl—the command simply hadn't been needed. Pal was gentle, outgoing, and friendly, and acting angry wasn't in his nature. Still, thinking better of the omission, Weatherwax soon introduced the snarl into his repertoire.

MGM, however, preferred the heroic yet gentle image of the snarl-free Lassie and played it up in several press releases. "Lassie knows more than 100 different commands," the studio declared, "but he is simply too nice and too polite to snarl. Lassie can swim rivers, climb mountains, lead children home from the woods, and carry a baby chick in his mouth, but if a scene requires him to snarl, the director must bring on a stunt dog." Pure and virtuous—and certainly no murderer—Lassie and his good name remained unsullied.

This sketch by Norman Rockwell entitled Murder Mystery depicts Lassie among an all-star line-up at the scene of a dire murder. The illustration, created for the Saturday Evening Post but never published, featured such stars as (left to right) Loretta Young, Ethel Barrymore, Richard Widmark, Linda Darnell, Boris Karloff, Clifton Webb — and, of course, Lassie.

The tremendous success of Pal and Rudd Weatherwax was celebrated in this color spread from a 1946 Saturday Evening Post. As the magazine observed, "It couldn't happen to a nicer dog."

When MGM had first spent $10,000 on the motion picture and marketing rights for *Lassie Come Home,* the studio hadn't expected its modest investment to become a hit. As originally conceived, *Lassie* was supposed to be a kids' movie, the kind of film that would entrance children while keeping their parents and grandparents interested, if not enthralled. While the script was well written and the actors were solid, the movie was not expected to win awards or make millions of dollars, and while its Technicolor images presented the most beautiful outdoor scenes since *Trail of the Lonesome Pine,* it wasn't even supposed to be particularly noteworthy as an outdoor epic. But now it had gained Mayer's support, and that was usually enough to ensure solid box-office.

Perhaps the person with the most to gain from *Lassie Come Home's* success was the dog's trainer. Rudd Weatherwax knew that this movie was his big break. *Lassie* gave him a unique vehicle to showcase all that he had learned in twenty years of training dogs for the movies. If he did a great job, it could do wonders for his new training facility. He also felt that this film would give Pal a chance to earn a special spot in movie history as one of the best canine performers. Still, even considering all the ramifications for himself and his animal, Weatherwax didn't expect the film to be anything more than a modest success. As he wrote in his book *The Story of Lassie*, "The film lacked the star names generally considered essential to box-office success. It had neither glamorous sex appeal nor intrigue."

As is so often the case when unexpected prosperity graces a modest vision, timing had a lot to do with *Lassie*'s strong reception. With the United States at war and bombs filling the skies of

"Wasn't my agent supposed to have called by now? What does he think I'm paying him for?"

The most famous publicity photo used in Lassie Come Home *shows Lassie with a napping Roddy McDowall.*

Europe and the Pacific, the public hungered for an escape from bad news and worry. A fresh draft of sentimental medicine was in order, and it came around the neck of a gold-and-white collie.

Yet timing alone didn't account for all of Lassie's good fortune. What made the movie really work, and what had made location filming relatively easy, was Rudd Weatherwax and his exceptional dog. As Eric Knight had quickly sensed when he saw master and animal toiling on the movie set, this duo was remarkable. Between them there was a power at work that seemed almost psychic. When a stunt was being played out, their minds seemed to be one. The magic was so striking that the dog fascinated and

How Lassie Came Home

*T*he most famous scene in *Lassie Come Home* comes at the very end of the film when, after her long journey across Scotland and England, Lassie limps into the schoolyard and waits for her master to get out of class.

What would happen after that, however, inspired much debate. Rudd Weatherwax thought that when Lassie saw Roddy McDowall's character, the dog should heroically struggle to her feet, slowly limp up to the boy, and lick his face. This would be the natural thing for the dog to do, he argued; the shocked boy would naturally wait for the dog to complete the journey, not move toward her himself.

But the film's director, Fred Wilcox, disagreed. He wanted the boy to pause when he saw Lassie and then race up to hug her. Then, as he bent down, Lassie would softly lay her head across the lad's knee and he would exclaim, "My Lassie has come home!"

This ending, the director argued, would provoke more emotion. Both versions were considered, but the trainer finally lost his battle, and today, five decades later, millions of fans agree that Wilcox's version of the scene is one of the most poignant ever filmed.

The homecoming scene from Lassie Come Home.

THE
PICTURE
THAT'S
TRUE
TO LIFE!

thrilled the experienced crew in a way that few human stars ever had. And if these veterans were so enthralled during their long hours of grueling work, anyone had to figure that what they were capturing on film was remarkable indeed. Just before the release of *Lassie Come Home*, yet another publicity tour was staged. This time Rudd, who had always worked behind the scenes, suddenly found himself front and center with his latest discovery by his side. As he paraded Pal before the media and put the dog through a number of difficult routines for their benefit, he was asked question after question about the dog who had so charmed MGM's lion, Mr. Mayer.

All the attention paid to Pal's talents and IQ amused the trainer, but some of the questions were disturbing. More than queries about the dog's innate acting abilities, Rudd was forced to respond to concerns about how the dog accomplished difficult stunts without being mistreated or abused. The media were looking for dirt, for even a hint of inhumane cruelty. They couldn't believe a dog would do voluntarily what Pal did in the movie. And so with great patience Rudd explained the tricks of the trade, from camera angles to rewards.

"When Lassie limped, we simply put a small piece of cork on his foot. This didn't hurt him, but it caused him to favor one side. The blood you

The title card from Lassie's debut. Note that Elizabeth Taylor did not earn star billing in this film.

45

When Pal became a real star even the finest hotels like the Waldorf-Astoria welcomed him. Of course he still had to sign in and promise not to howl after midnight.

saw was actually catsup." (In this case the biggest trick was keeping Pal from licking it off.)

"When Lassie looks as if he is fighting," Rudd continued, "he is actually playing. The dogs in these play fights are friends who know each other well and play as any dogs do. We make sure that there is no way either of them can get hurt."

On and on Rudd went, and the explanations were repeated every time someone saw a preview. No one, it seemed, believed that a trainer could do what Rudd did without abusing the dog.

Fortunately for Rudd, his positive reward-and-praise techniques were readily endorsed by the SPCA officials who worked the MGM set during the shoot.

In mid-October 1943, Rudd and Pal made a final swing to the East Coast, accompanied by some of the other *Lassie* stars. The emphasis of this final publicity junket was the premiere of the film at Radio City Music Hall. As enthusiastic as their early reception had been, the troupe of players and crew were totally unprepared for the press and public reaction to the event. An air of special excitement enveloped all of New York as thousands turned out to greet the canine star. Every ticket was sold at premium prices and every major paper had its reviewer there covering the opening. Louis B. Mayer's publicity machine had churned out a winner. Now if only the movie could live up to the advance interest.

When the evening of the premiere finally arrived, a finely dressed audience filed inside to see what had been done with the best-selling book. The house lights were lowered, the Technicolor images of the now highly hyped film filled the screen, and the crowd grew quiet. As the movie unfolded, few in the audience left their seats even for popcorn or a rest-room break. Sniffles could be heard throughout the house, for the dog's performance seemed to affect every viewer's emotions. When it was over the audience, overcome by the same emotions that had moved Louis B. Mayer to tears, arose en masse to give the film and its cast a thunderous standing ovation. Their reaction confirmed what the film executive had surmised—this was by no means just another dog story, and Pal was by no means just another dog.

The reviews were tremendous. Some dubbed *Lassie Come Home* one of the best films of 1943—"or any other year," one critic said. The cast all earned high marks, as did director Wilcox and the wonderful location photography. People loved Roddy McDowall and they were awed by young Elizabeth Taylor's beauty, but what really caught the critics' attention was not the humans in the film. Once a motorcycle-chasing orphan, Pal had stolen the show. If he had been able to read the newspapers—and by now many people were convinced he could—he would have blushed, especially at one review that called him "Greer Garson in furs."

By the time the West Coast premiere took place, Lassie was a real star. And to emphasize that fact, almost every one of Tinsel Town's dogs, including Rin Tin Tin, Asta, and Daisy, were there at the premiere to greet him. Yet even as MGM counted the more than $3 million they had made during the film's first weekend of release, even as flashbulbs popped and the media barked questions, Rudd sensed that this streak of good fortune wouldn't continue.

Still, as the spotlight hit the formally dressed trainer and his well-groomed star, as hundreds cheered (or barked), as Rudd's and Pal's pictures traveled by wire service across the nation and around the world, the dog seemed to savor the moment. Some thought they saw him smile, and why not? For in a city full of stars, his was, for the moment, the brightest. It is said that every dog shall have his day, and surely this was Pal's.

Dog Days in Tinsel Town:
Lassie Hits the Big Screen

espite Rudd Weatherwax's pessimism, by Christmas MGM's offices were being deluged with mail asking when another *Lassie* movie was going to be made. Soon the public quit asking for another film and began to demand one. Thousands inquired if they could have "pawtographed" pictures of Lassie, and even more wanted to buy one of Lassie's pups. On the road, Weatherwax and Pal were drawing multitudes everywhere they went. Some trains were now even letting Pal ride in the passenger section, although he still wasn't allowed to eat in the diner. On the strength of one movie appearance, the talented canine was as popular as any human star and a great deal easier to handle.

For younger fans, Pal was Hollywood's very best movie star. At fairs and rodeos the kids turned out in record numbers just to see him go through a ten-minute routine. Besides the usual sit-up-and-beg dog tricks, Pal re-created his heart-winning river scene, choosing a child from the audience to "come home" to and then laying his head in the lucky child's lap—an experience not soon to be forgotten. In little more than a year, Pal had gone from being unwanted to being the most popular dog in the world.

So it shouldn't have been completely unexpected that early in 1944 Weatherwax was asked to meet with the executives at MGM, who were interested in making a follow-up picture. In order to keep their top dog and their best trainer happy they tore up Pal's first contract and offered Rudd a new one, this time with a five-year non-option clause. He and his dog would earn $500 a month during the filming of all future *Lassie* movies. In addition, the studio agreed to pay the duo $300 monthly even when they were not needed for film or publicity work (the usual canine pay scale at this time was at best $25 a week). For a dog trainer, this five-year deal offered unheard-of long-range security. As good as this arrangement was, however, MGM would tear it up several times over the next few years and increase those generous numbers. After two decades in the business, Rudd had become an overnight success.

Meanwhile in faraway Africa, Eric Knight was involved in the day-to-day rigors of the war. He was serving his country by writing and filming the real sounds of battle for Frank Capra's *Why We*

Previous page: Arguably the most handsome male and most beautiful female leads at MGM, Pal and his costar in Courage of Lassie.

Fight series. While he had been back in the States he had kept up with the filming of his book, but since the movie's release he had been involved in the war effort overseas and had been unable to see the film. Then, in January 1944, his plane went down on a flight to Cairo. At the age of forty-five, Lassie's creator had died, never realizing the scope of the legend he had helped establish.

As it would turn out, *Lassie Come Home* was just the first of many successes for Pal and Lassie. The year before Rudd transformed Pal into Lassie, the Weatherwaxes had grossed $14,000 between the training school and their work in motion pictures. Starting the moment Lassie climbed out of the San Joaquin River, their gross for the next twelve months hit $50,000. The following year it rose higher, and within a few more years Lassie's salary alone had passed that figure.

The Weatherwax kennel of working movie dogs had grown, too. When Rudd placed Pal in *Lassie Come Home,* only a few dogs were kept at the brothers' school full-time. Two years later that number had grown to more than seventy, and those seventy worked so consistently that the brothers had almost twenty assistants just to train the animals and get them to their shoots. None of them had the star qualities of Pal, but movie viewers were seeing them as background players almost every day.

As the fan letters rolled in and the pawtographs were shipped out, Louis B. Mayer became so high on Pal/Lassie that he ordered the dog's image added to MGM's gallery of motion-picture artists. The mogul often bragged that this roster contained "the greatest array of stars in Hollywood." In 1945 the list began with June Allyson and Fred Astaire, ran through names like Gable, Garson, and Tracy, and ended with Esther Williams. About halfway down the long row of color portraits, right between Hedy Lamarr and

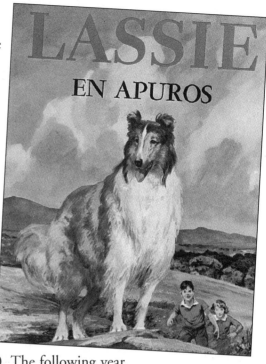

Lassie's cinematic success created an audience for kids' books about the famous dog. This is a Spanish-language edition of a Big Golden Book, now prized by Lassie collectors.

Myrna Loy, was Lassie. Lana Turner may have been discovered in a drugstore, but Pal went her one better. He was discovered in a river, and MGM made sure that the public was informed of this time and again. MGM also capitalized on the fact that Lassie was not a registered dog. The studio wanted most of its stars to have a "regular guy" image. They could be glamorous at a dinner or a show, but underneath that facade Mayer felt that the public would more quickly embrace someone who through talent, grit, determination, and luck became a star. Such a persona was created for Pal/Lassie by portraying him as an unwanted puppy, a dog without papers, a canine in need of love and attention who rose to the river's challenge and outshone the most nobly bred animal. Constantly, MGM reminded fans that their star was a great deal like the dog they had in their own backyards—a part of the magic of Lassie was getting consumers to believe that if the Fates had acted otherwise, Lassie might have been *their* dog.

To keep this wholesome, all-American image front-stage and center, Pal and Rudd went on the road and met the fans face-to-face. Rudd answered the questions about what Lassie ate—"stew"—what he drank—"water"—and what he liked to do—"play, just like any other dog." He explained that for Pal, filming movies or doing shows was playing. The trainer also told and re-told the story of having been given Pal by a man who thought he was untrainable. He encouraged fans to go to their local animal shelters and see if they could discover the next great movie dog.

Rudd and Pal never seemed to tire of meeting their adoring fans. Once, while visiting a park, Rudd left Pal with a group of children while he went to get something to drink. When he came back, he was horrified to discover that the children were scissoring off the dog's hair. If Rudd had arrived any later, his star might have been in need of a good toupee. Grinning, the trainer pried his animal away from the kids and considered how far they had come in such a short while.

Unlikely as it sounds, Lassie was also a guest on radio shows. A simple bark over a microphone was all that was needed to make ratings soar. A comedian would make a dog joke, Pal would groan,

and the audience would laugh. When someone told a sad story, the dog would cry. Eventually he even had his own radio show, from 1946 to 1949. Of course Pal did little more than bark, whine, and cry. The sound people did most of the work, creating the fight scenes and all other necessary acoustic effects, while an announcer kept the listener informed of what the dog was doing and a few human actors filled in with the dialogue. Over the air it sounded perfect, so good that no one seemed to realize that Rudd was there giving his dog hand signals every step of the way. To the listener, Lassie was a genius.

MGM had latched on to a phenomenon, one they didn't fully understand. The one thing they *did* realize was that they had to get Pal back in front of the camera before all of this hysteria died. They rushed out a script for a film called *Son of Lassie,* which was something of a continuation of Knight's original story. In it,

MGM lined up fifty-eight of its greatest performers for this 1949 family photograph, including such stars as Clark Gable, Katharine Hepburn, Frank Sinatra, Errol Flynn, June Allyson, Judy Garland, and Fred Astaire.

Peter Lawford and Pal hiding from Nazis in Son of Lassie.

Joe, the boy Lassie traveled the length of Britain to find, has now grown up and happens to look a great deal like matinée idol Peter Lawford. Joe is now a member of the English air corps and actively involved in fighting the Nazis. His beloved dog, Laddie, hitches a ride on his bomber and they crash; the two of them then cross Europe together, fighting the enemy while attempting to get back to England. In this sequel, Priscilla, the part that Elizabeth Taylor had originated just over a year before, was turned over to a young and spunky June Lockhart. Her role in the film was to help take care of Laddie's mother, Lassie, and wait for her Joe to return.

As this plot synopsis suggests, the main character in *Son of Lassie* was not Lassie but her son Laddie. And in this regard a bit of very unique casting occurred. Pal stepped out of the role that had made him a star, turning the part of Lassie over to another Weatherwax collie, and instead he played the lead, Laddie. Somehow the

switch never fazed the public. Most of them seemed to notice that the dog they thought of as Lassie was now playing a male, but few seemed to care.

Besides the three cast changes involving Lassie, Lawford, and Lockhart, by and large the rest of the cast of *Son of Lassie* looked much like the original, except this time there were literally hundreds of collies on the set. "In one scene," Weatherwax reported, "we had fifty of the most valuable show champions of the region making their debut before the cameras. The total value of the group was approximated at $100,000, with several of the dogs be-

Peter Lawford was a matinee idol and Pal was already a big-name MGM star, but at the time Son of Lassie was being filmed, June Lockhart was a young actress in search of a big break.

ing appraised at $10,000 apiece. They were blue ribbon winners from all parts of the country—from North Hollywood to New York's Madison Square Garden."

Just after the opening credits of *Son of Lassie* this group of dogs came racing over a hill. They filled the screen with all shapes and varieties of the best of the collie breed. Yet even with all their ribbons and their titles, none could do for their breed what the unwanted, pet-quality Pal had already done.

In 1944 only 2,721 purebred collie puppies were registered in the United States. This figure had been stable dating back to the 1920s. Not even Albert Payson Terhune's great collie novels, including *Lad, a Dog*, had created much of a surge in collie breeding and buying. In the eyes of most Americans, the collie was generally seen as high-strung and hard to work with, for the dogs had been labeled with the inaccurate reputation of being spoiled and unsuited for families. It was generally agreed that their place was out in the country, herding sheep and goats. With the release of *Lassie Come Home* this perception dramatically changed. Thanks to the on-screen image of Pal/Lassie, by 1946 there were 10,463 registrations, a gain of nearly 300 percent, and the number would double over the next three years. Across the border in Canada the collie jumped from out of nowhere to become the nation's favorite breed during this same time period.

Lassie's tremendous popularity became very evident to director Fred Wilcox on one occasion when he was filming a military-dog-training scene in a Los Angeles park. A large number of children had gathered just out of camera range to watch Lassie jump moats, scale fences, and fight Nazis. To their dismay, however, the script called for the dog to fail every one of these tests and prove unworthy of military work, so Pal failed as he was directed. For the kids it was like seeing Babe Ruth strike out four straight times with the bases loaded. Disillusioned, they began to drift mournfully away. Sensing what was happening, Wilcox halted shooting and asked Rudd to show the youngsters what their Lassie could really do. Pal performed perfectly, of course, and his image was saved.

While Los Angeles locations and studio lots were used for some shots, most of *Son of Lassie* was filmed on Vancouver Island, just off the coast of British Columbia, and along the mountain trails and glaciers of the Canadian Rockies. As they had done for the location shots in the first movie, cast and crew traveled by train to the sites. But this time Pal was allowed out of the baggage car and moved into first-class. He was now considered a real star, and the railroad gave him all the privileges that accompanied stardom. He could sleep in a Pullman, eat in the diner, and go anywhere he wanted when the train was moving. He wasn't even required to be on a leash.

Most of the setups for this film were done in remote wilderness areas. The cast and crew often had to walk miles just to get to the expanse deemed the most dramatic and photogenic. Still, no matter how difficult the trek, no matter how bad the weather, no matter what time of day, there were always scores of fans who would track down the MGM production crew to seek out Weatherwax and his dog. Most brought cameras and asked for the now famous pawtographs. By the time the shooting closed and the cast and crew were ready to return home, Lassie had posed for the camera with more than 4,000 fans, from children to top government officials to troops from the Royal Canadian Mounted Police.

Rudd was amazed that his dog could stir such admiration. But one warm Canadian day he observed an encounter that helped him understand just what Lassie's special qualities were.

"We were at a veterans' hospital," Rudd recalled, "and after Lassie's show at the hospital we made a tour of the wards where the most serious patients had been unable to leave their beds to see him perform. Because we already

Pal listens in with the film's sound men during location shooting in the Canadian Rockies for Son of Lassie.

were late for our next scheduled stop, it had to be a quick tour, with Lassie just pausing briefly in each ward. However, as we passed one bed, which held an older man, Lassie took matters into his own paws. Turning from his place at my side, he went over to the bed, made a deep bow by it, and then, squatting down, put his paws up on the edge where the patient could touch him. I let him stay as long as we could, while the man, with tears in his eyes, stroked Lassie lovingly and talked to him.

"From a nurse in the ward, I later learned that this veteran, who had been a hospital patient ever since being wounded in World War I, had taken a turn for the worse and was not expected to live until the next day. How Lassie understood that, I wouldn't pretend to know. Yet I am certain that he felt the closeness of death. His response to it provided a remarkable and touching insight into dog's natural regard for man."

Rudd, who already knew that Pal was the most talented dog he had ever owned, now realized that he was also the most perceptive. It was probably the combination of these two qualities that allowed the dog to react to emotions and situations in a way that made him a true actor. The audience believed this performer because he seemed to behave in a way that said, "I believe this is real, too." Somehow, his expression could register the full range of emotions. He sensed what was needed and he gave it. Yet as rare as these qualities were, by themselves they couldn't make him "the world's greatest dog star." There had to be something else.

That "something else" became clear on a grueling day of appearances during the Canadian trip—a day Weatherwax once said filled him with the greatest pride he ever felt for Pal. They had stopped in Vancouver, en route from Victoria to Banff, to make personal appearances requested and arranged by Canadian army officers. From early morning until nightfall, Pal made the rounds of military installations, training camps, and hospitals in the city and its suburbs. Everywhere he went, Pal—or Lassie, as the fans called him—put on a real show for the men and women in uniform. By the time he arrived at his last stop—the army headquarters in the center of the city—the trainer could tell that his dog

Oceangoing Hero

On screen, Pal made his living by acting out heroic rescues of everything from lambs to squadrons of soldiers, but in real life skeptics had to wonder—how much of a hero *was* the real Lassie? Pal could walk the walk, but could he talk the talk?

The answer came when Pal and Rudd Weatherwax were spending the night off Catalina Island on Lassie's own boat, the *Lassie*, an oceangoing vessel that could sleep four. Lying on deck after his master had gone to bed, Pal began to bark, and he wouldn't stop until Rudd came to investigate. Shaking himself awake, the trainer climbed up the steps and out onto the deck.

"What is it, boy?" he asked.

Pal walked to the boat's side and Rudd followed, peering out into the darkness. "I don't see anything," he muttered as he studied his dog, but as he turned to go back to bed, Pal began to bark again and look out at the water.

Scratching his brow, Rudd returned to the dog's side and listened to the waves softly hitting the side of the boat. Then, ever so faintly, he heard what sounded like a human voice.

Turning on the engine and pulling up anchor, he guided the boat in the direction of the cries. But after a little more than a minute he cut the motor, unable to pick up the voices over the mechanical hum, and returned to Pal's side.

"I hear them, boy," Rudd assured the dog. "They're somewhere out there in the fog." He listened to the cries again to determine their direction and moved back to the wheel. But as he looked forward he noticed that Pal was standing in the front, occasionally moving a few feet to his right as he looked out over the water. Using Pal as a compass, he steered the boat through the thick fog, cutting the engine only when he saw the dog's tail swishing wildly.

Grabbing his flashlight, Rudd ran to the bow and looked out over the water. There for the first time he saw a small boat drifting helplessly without lights or power, and three people aboard who were very glad to see the furry face that went with that faraway bark. Tossing them a line, Rudd towed them back to port.

The U. S. Coast Guard awarded Pal their "Certificate of Honor" for his part in saving those lives. On or off screen, it was one of the dog's finest moments.

Pal won admirers in Canada during the filming of Son of Lassie, appearing on a Vancouver street to help with a Red Cross donation drive.

was quite tired. But as they drove up to the building, Rudd saw a sight that he would never forget. This was the only one of the day's appearances that had been announced in the Vancouver newspapers, and jamming the streets of the city's busiest intersection, stopping traffic in all directions, was a crowd that must have numbered close to ten thousand.

A special detachment of soldiers and policemen met the car and cleared a way through the throng. With great difficulty they made a lane for Pal to a flat-bed truck. As the crowd pressed closely around the impromptu stage, the exhausted Pal gave his best performance of the day. According to Rudd, as soon as Pal saw all the fans he perked up and looked as fresh as he had been when he had started out early that morning. He pranced around the truck's platform, shaking hands with the children who managed to reach its edge and giving several of them a "kiss" before he went through his jumps and other routines. At that point Rudd knew that this dog was born to be an actor. He fed off the audience, and he loved to perform.

When away from the crowd or the cameras, Pal would grow restless. He liked attention, and he always seemed to want to learn new routines. Unlike some animals who would perform only if they knew a treat was coming, Pal would work for nothing but attention. If he wasn't getting enough of that at home, he would go into a routine on his own just to make sure everyone knew he was around.

In addition to his acting career, the gentle Pal also served as four-year-old Robert Weatherwax's baby-sitter. He made sure that the boy didn't wander too far from home or family. If he did, Pal would gently grab the boy's arm or hand and lead him back to where the dog felt he would be safe. He did the same thing with kittens, bunnies, and almost all other "helpless" creatures. In short, Pal was very much like the sensitive, caring animal he always played—he was just more talented.

Everyone who worked with Pal recognized his talents. Elizabeth Taylor and Roddy McDowall loved him, Donald Crisp thought that he was Strongheart reborn, Peter Lawford admitted that he had never met such a scene-stealer, and Louis B. Mayer thought of him as one of his greatest stars. But some thought the credit should go from the dog back to his trainer.

"Pal was a remarkable dog," agreed June Lockhart, his costar in *Son of Lassie*, "but Rudd and those who worked with him were even more remarkable. They could make everything the dog did look so unrehearsed. Yet it wasn't; they had planned out the action step by step. That is what made Pal look so wonderfully smart on the screen."

June, whose parents had both been well known on the English stage, had grown up in America but still had enough of a British accent to be teased for it at school. Yet it was the way she spoke, coupled with her ladylike manners, that allowed her to beat out Ava Gardner for the part in *Son of Lassie*. Even as she signed the contract and reviewed the script, however, she knew that the film's real star was not a beautiful young woman but a dog. It didn't bother her a bit. Like the children in the park, it was a treat just to watch Rudd and the dog work. "In a scene where the puppy Laddie was supposed to pull my skirt off, Rudd hid a small bit of meat in the hem of the skirt," she explained years later, obviously still impressed by the stunt. "He had it sewn in. The puppy smelled the meat and gave the skirt a good yank. After several solid tugs, it came right off. It was a great tribute to Rudd and Sam Williamson [one of Weatherwax's associates] as well as those who worked with them, that they could always figure a way to make the dog look as if he understood everything that was going on."

On the train ride back from the Canadian location filming, Peter Lawford, who had been hired for the movie because of his teen appeal, had spent a great deal of time playing with Pal. As he did, he noted a young boy watching him. The boy's eyes followed all of Pal's actions. Finally, after several hours of scrutinizing the dog and the actor from a distance, the child worked up the courage to approach Lawford.

"Do you know Lassie?" the child shyly inquired.

"Sure do. I get to work with him almost every day," Lawford answered as he folded his arms and smiled. Surely now the child would recognize him and ask for an autograph.

The boy, his eyes filled with wonder, frowned, and then asked the actor, "How much do you have to pay to do that?"

Shaking his head, Lawford realized something June Lockhart had known all along. This was Lassie's picture and no one else's.

To the surprise of few, *Son of Lassie* was another big box-office success. The word around Tinsel Town was that Lassie would indeed come home, time and time again, and when he walked in the door he would always carry with him a great deal of money. In MGM's case this was certainly true. Some even suggested that the company retire Leo the Lion, its longtime trademark, and replace him with Lassie, the real king of film.

Leo kept his job, but maybe only because the studio could better use Lassie in other capacities. Besides working on a number of new Technicolor vehicles for their star, MGM lined him up with personal appearances all over the nation. They made sure that he was spoiled and pampered, but they also made sure that he was working.

Pal's picture was also now gracing every can of Red Heart dog food. "Lassie thrives on Red Heart," the ad copy read. "If your dog deserves the best, why not give him the food that is good enough for a movie star?" Tens of thousands of cases were sold all around the country so that everyone's everyday Fido could get Lassie's dinner each night. Of course Pal was still eating beef stew, but the public didn't need to know that.

Pal's personal appearance fees were exceeded only by those of

stars like Frank Sinatra, Bing Crosby, and a few big band leaders, but he still couldn't fulfill all the requests. He earned $1,500 for just two nights of shows in San Francisco, and a few months later the price had climbed to $2,000 for two days at a dog show in Detroit. He became a highly paid semi-regular on the stages of the Oriental Theatre in Chicago and the Orpheum in Los Angeles, with a schedule so tight that Rudd purchased a private plane to fly him to his various obligations. Pal/Lassie also had his own bedroom and a boat. He rode in limos and drank bottled water while on the road. He was as much a star as Bogart and Bacall, and he probably had a larger loyal following than either of these rival Warner Bros.'s players.

Pal and Elizabeth Taylor studying during a break in the filming of Courage of Lassie.

Following on the success of the first two Lassie movies, in 1946 MGM released *Courage of Lassie*, which featured Liz Taylor. This effort, again directed by Fred Wilcox, was based on the exploits of a famous war dog and was filmed on location in Canada. The Lassie name in the title had nothing to do with the movie—it was merely a reflection of what MGM thought it took to sell a dog film. This time Pal played Bill, Liz's lost puppy who ends up in the army. Early in the film, Carl "Alfalfa" Switzer (from the *Our Gang* series) accidentally shoots the puppy, and Liz nurses him back to health. But later she loses him and he becomes a hero in the war, fighting for the Allies. When he returns home shell-shocked, the townspeople think he is a menace and plan to put him down. Fortunately Frank Morgan, famous as the Wizard in *The Wizard of*

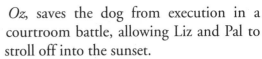

LASSIE thrives on RED HEART 3-FLAVOR Dog Food*

RED HEART

3-FLAVOR DOG FOOD

Like today's celebrities, Pal was an advertising star throughout the late forties.

Oz, saves the dog from execution in a courtroom battle, allowing Liz and Pal to stroll off into the sunset.

Courage of Lassie gave Pal a chance to play some great war scenes complete with exploding bombs, slippery mud, and pouring rain. He convincingly acted out being injured and then dragging himself to get help, performing like a real canine trooper and helping to educate many about the exploits of real war dogs. Sentimental, warm, and filled with enough action to satisfy both children and adults, the film pleased both the critics and the fans. Besides, it featured a young woman who was already becoming more than an actress. Even at the tender age of fourteen, it was obvious that Elizabeth Taylor, like Pal, had an enormous amount of star quality. (Another of this film's interesting background players was George Cleveland, who would, some eight years later, help establish Lassie's reign on television.)

The next Lassie release, *Hills of Home,* reunited the dog with Edmund Gwenn, who had appeared in *Lassie Come Home.* This 1948 picture presented a sentimental tale of an old Scottish doctor and a dog he saves from a cruel master. The outdoor drama used the Sonora Pass in the California High Sierras as a backdrop, and, as always, the Technicolor images made the picture seem bigger than life. Donald Crisp was also back, joined by a young Janet Leigh and Tom Drake. Pal's biggest challenge in this picture was to behave as if he were scared of water. Actually, Pal was a wonderful swimmer, and he loved to play in ponds, rivers, and swimming pools. The mere fact that he appears to be so frightened of water in this picture points out just how good he and Rudd both were. As could be predicted, the plot of *Hills of Home* required that the dog lose his fear in order to save the day. Be assured that he did.

The reviews for *Hills of Home* were solid, the sales good, and Pal was as wonderful as ever, but the essence of what had been Eric Knight's Lassie was now all but forgotten. No longer was this a story of a child and his dog. No longer was Lassie fighting the elements to return to his master's side. Now he was a misunderstood animal with a simple agenda. The movie was still first-rate entertainment, but the studio had begun to veer drastically from Knight's original vision of Lassie.

A year later, Lassie returned to the screen with film legend Jeanette MacDonald in *The Sun Comes Up*. Written especially for Lassie by Marjorie Kinnan Rawlings, the film staged its biggest coup by landing Claude Jarman, Jr., as the juvenile lead. Jarman, widely acclaimed for his work in *The Yearling* (the film version of

Hills of Home featured an impressive cast, including a young Janet Leigh as well as Pal's old pals Edmund Gwenn and Donald Crisp. The plot involved a dog overcoming his fear of water in order to save his master.

Lassie and Liz

Over the years two myths have arisen concerning film legend Elizabeth Taylor and the movie *Lassie Come Home*. The first is that *Lassie Come Home* was the violet-eyed youngster's first film part. Actually, before Lassie *Come Home* she had appeared in the 1942 picture *There's One Born Every Minute*. The second and most enduring myth is that the beautiful young girl was the film's big star. In truth the movie's posters and press releases listed seven performers as the picture's stars, none of them Liz: Lassie, Roddy McDowall, Donald Crisp, Dame May Whitty, Edmund Gwenn, Nigel Bruce, and Elsa Lanchester. Liz's name appeared nowhere in publicity releases or lead credits, and even when the film was rereleased in the early 1970s she was left off the bill. Liz's few minutes on the screen, which primarily consisted of hugging Lassie, were not enough to rate the young girl star billing.

Taylor was just another child actress attempting to prove her worth at this point, one of many talented young girls who were a part of a Hollywood studio machine that included Judy Garland, June Lockhart, and Natalie Wood. But while she wasn't the star of *Lassie Come Home*, the film gave her the exposure she needed to land the lead in *National Velvet*, her fifth film and the one that made her a real star.

What seems to have confused generations of Liz watchers is that the actress did eventually share star billing with the famous dog in her sixth film. With *Courage of Lassie*, at fourteen years old, Liz finally earned top billing with her costar.

Fifty years after the collie and the beautiful young girl got their starts, real stars have become virtually a thing of the past. But just as Lassie and Liz began their climb to the top together, so too do they remain together, the last of the great movie stars.

Elizabeth and Pal.

Pal was as gentle as a lamb on and off the set. Here he and Liz herd sheep in Courage of Lassie.

Rawling's Pulitzer Prize–winning novel), was a hot property. By combining the child's appeal with Lassie and MacDonald, MGM felt that this sentimental story of an orphan and a widow would light up the box office. For the most part, however, it was too sweet and predictable. Here we have a widow blaming a dog for the death of a child. As one might guess, the dog withstands much abuse in order to redeem himself by the end through heroic actions. While *The Sun Comes Up* made money, it did not capture the public's imagination as the first four Lassie movies had. Part of the blame for the "can't miss" film's misfire may have been the absence of Fred Wilcox. For the first time in his career, Pal didn't have the director who had helped make him a star.

Offscreen, MGM continued to expand Lassie's influence, launching a line of children's books, publishing a comic book featuring Lassie's worldwide travels, and introducing Lassie puzzles. With Knight's original book having been translated into a score of languages and published in a range of editions, MGM also pushed Lassie overseas. Still, to keep mining gold from the dog's name, the studio needed another hit movie.

In order to restore Lassie to the status of a top-flight star, MGM purchased the rights to Eleanor Atkinson's well-known dog story *Greyfriars Bobby*, which the studio renamed *Challenge to Lassie* to make sure they fully realized just who was starring. They also reunited the dog with Edmund Gwenn and Donald Crisp,

Jeanette MacDonald dumped Nelson Eddy for MGM's brightest new stars, Claude Jarman, Jr., and Pal, in *The Sun Comes Up*.

By the time Pal made The Sun Comes Up, he rated star treatment in every possible way. And one look at the chairs or the scripts proved he was an equal with any of his human costars.

and added the distinguished veteran player Alan Napier, best known for his later role as Alfred the butler on television's *Batman.* The location was returned to the High Sierras, and for added insurance the studio loaded the cast with cute kids.

Like few other outdoor films released in 1950, this movie worked. The performances were solid, Lassie was given a role that he and his trainer could sink their teeth into, and the story had the emotion that had been missing since the first two Lassie efforts. Here Lassie played a small-town dog whose owner had died. The mourning dog sleeps by his master's grave each night, but because he has no master he is ruled a stray and ordered put to sleep. The children of the town come to his rescue, and his wish, to remain by his master's side, is granted. Like the first two Lassie movies, this plot has a sentimental feel enhanced by rich character acting, talent, and a solid group of stunts. Still, times were changing; the days of contract players were all but over, and hero dogs and maudlin story lines were losing their following.

The studio's last Lassie effort, *The Painted Hills,* was just another dog adventure, this time set in the mining days of the Old West. Lassie played Shep, a dog whose owner dies and who is then

This lobby card from <u>Challenge to Lassie</u> depicts a scene in which the dog's beloved old owner (Donald Crisp) warns his pet to stay off the streets while he performs his errands. All the MGM lobby cards and movie posters were hand colored, but for some reason Pal was always left in black and white.

In court Edmund Gwenn pleads Lassie's case as the dog tries to assure the courtroom that he is not just a stray animal.

adopted by a young boy. Into the plot is tossed a gold mine, a greedy villain, some Indians, and a chase across vast and scenic wilderness. But in truth this cross between a western and a dog movie was a B picture. The stars that MGM tossed in were practically unknown and weren't even listed on the film's lobby cards and posters. *The Painted Hills* was truly the dog's vehicle, and his fame had to carry the burden of box-office success. Although it was publicized as Lassie's "most exciting" film, it did not receive big money backing or a great publicity push from MGM. Of all the MGM Lassie movies, only this one didn't live up to the high standards set by Louis B. Mayer.

A Lassie Is a Lassie Is a Lassie

*F*ans have long been confused by the different dogs who served as Lassie over the years, but that's only half the jumble of nameology. Other stars whose work appealed to kids usually played themselves—Roy Rogers always played Roy, Gene Autry played Gene—but in the movies the dog fans knew as Lassie rarely appeared as a character named Lassie. True, in the very first Lassie outing, *Lassie Come Home*, Pal was featured as Lassie. But in *Son of Lassie* he stepped out of the role and played a dog named Laddie while one of Pal's relatives played Lassie, Laddie's mom.

As confusing as that sounds, it gets even more complicated. In the next film, *Courage of Lassie*, Pal appears as a dog Liz Taylor's character has named Bill. Throughout the movie Pal plays Bill, although of course the credits list Lassie as playing Bill. For accuracy's sake they probably should have read, "Pal playing Lassie playing Bill." But what was the name Lassie doing in the title anyway? After all, no studio would create a movie called *Courage of John Wayne* and then have the Duke play a character named Max.

In Pal's, or Lassie's, next movie, *Hills of Home*, the lead dog has no real name, although throughout the picture Pal is referred to as Lass or Girl. The Lassie name was also dropped from the title of *The Sun Comes Up*, and Lassie/Pal finished his MGM days by playing a dog named Shep in *The Painted Hills*.

As had now become all too obvious to Weatherwax, Pal was just another actor finishing out his contract. MGM's focus was elsewhere as the Hollywood moguls suspiciously eyed a new fad—television. Sensing that kids would now get their entertainment from a tube, the studio opted to go after the adult audience. Despite the fact that MGM had ridden the collie for a reported quarter of a billion dollars in receipts, they now were ready to put him out to kennel. For Pal the movie star, it was probably time to retire. After all, he was pushing eleven years old. Rudd's highly publicized ten-dollar investment had paid off handsomely. Thanks to the Lassie movies, the trainer and some of his other dogs were being used by everyone from Disney to Warner's, and Rudd had enough

Pal played Shep in The Painted Hills, a dog who is thought to be just another dumb animal; only at the end, after defeating the villain and saving his young master, is his true glory revealed.

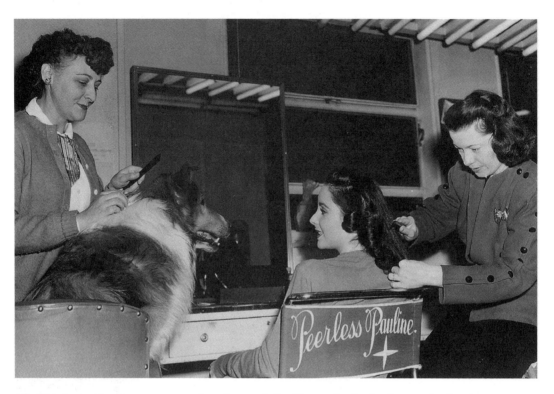

Liz Taylor and her friend Pal chat over old times at the hairdresser's.

money to last for a while. Yet, as he looked into the big brown eyes of what had become his best friend, he knew that he had to do one more thing for the dog and himself. Even though he couldn't have realized it then, this action would immortalize them both and forever haunt MGM.

Top Dog on Sunday Night:
Lassie Moves to TV

By 1951 MGM seemed to be finished with Pal. Unlike so many of their other has-been human actors, however, Pal and Rudd Weatherwax presented them with a unique problem—because the dog's contract was of the non-option type, they couldn't simply be released. Several times the contract had been rolled over and upgraded, and now the studio would have to pay the dog and Weatherwax for several more years, even if they didn't work. At this point MGM already owed the duo almost $40,000, and that figure was increasing each day they remained on the active contract list.

Unknown to the studio heads, Weatherwax was also tired of being on that list. He figured that if he could manage to own the Lassie name and trademark he could earn a nice income for at least three more years by traveling the country and appearing at shows, fairs, and rodeos. As long as he was tied to MGM, a big part of any appearance money had to be shared with the studio. The Lassie trademark would have to belong to Rudd in order to make working with Pal outside of movies worth his time.

Months went by with no new scripts submitted and none being considered. Hating to see money wasted on a used-up property, some of the studio's corporate lawyers tried to figure a way to break the dog's contract. Considering the problem too small to concern the higher-ups, they did so without checking with the board of directors. Around that time, Rudd approached the lawyers with his own buy-out offer. In the minds of the junior executives who were consulted, this was a gift from heaven. According to press accounts Weatherwax's offer involved renouncing any claim on the money he and Pal were or would be owed for all past and future work in exchange for all rights to the dog's name and trademark. The lawyers thought that the trainer had lost his mind—without film support, how could Lassie be worth $4,000, much less $40,000? They immediately drew up an agreement before Rudd had the time to regain his senses.

Rudd had recently written a successful book on Lassie, and from the sales he knew the dog was still popular. By trading off the Lassie name already made for him by the movies, he knew he could make the appearance money last for a few years. It made good

Previous page: Tom Rettig, Jan Clayton, George Miller, and Lassie, Jr., in an early publicity shot from Lassie. Reproduced in postcard form, this picture was sent out by Campbell's to everyone who wrote a fan letter to the show.

business sense. But sentimentally Rudd also wanted to own the rights to the Lassie name.

"He loved Pal, he loved what the image of Lassie had come to stand for, and he didn't want to see it fall into anyone's hands who could diminish that image," Robert Weatherwax explained. "By owning the trademark Dad knew that he had a way that Pal could go out with a dignity befitting the kind of dog he had been. In a very real sense, Dad owed Pal a great deal."

With all rights in hand, Rudd hit the road immediately. Pal

With Lassie, Jr., on the left, the aging Pal in the center, and Rudd Weatherwax on the right, the Lassie family lines up for a portrait at the Weatherwax home.

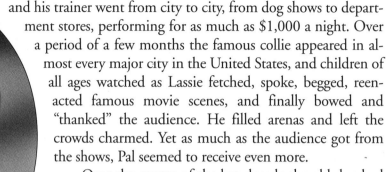

Tom Rettig was an experienced actor when he won the role of Jeff Miller. Before Lassie, the most famous blonde he had worked with was Marilyn Monroe on River of No Return.

and his trainer went from city to city, from dog shows to department stores, performing for as much as $1,000 a night. Over a period of a few months the famous collie appeared in almost every major city in the United States, and children of all ages watched as Lassie fetched, spoke, begged, reenacted famous movie scenes, and finally bowed and "thanked" the audience. He filled arenas and left the crowds charmed. Yet as much as the audience got from the shows, Pal seemed to receive even more.

Over the course of the last decade the old dog had grown to love performing. He sprang to life in front of a crowd and showed puppylike energy whenever he heard applause. Each night, with each new eighteen-minute show, the veteran trainer knew that he had done the right thing by letting Pal finish his career on the road. The dog couldn't have been happier, and the trainer couldn't have been prouder.

Rudd was not the only one who had noticed that there was still a great deal of life in the old dog. Bob Maxwell, a producer who understood the potential power of television, had watched as Lassie drew huge audiences for live shows, and he approached Weatherwax with an offer. The fledgling television networks were hungry for programming and Maxwell was convinced that a television show featuring a dog and a family would fill a niche that both viewers and advertisers couldn't help but love. The producer then proposed that he and Rudd form a partnership, locate a solid core of actors, come up with a suitable family story line, and shoot a pilot. If they both felt good about the final results, they would attempt to find a buyer among the four television networks: CBS, ABC, NBC, and DuMont.

Rudd was intrigued. When he had purchased the Lassie trademark from MGM he had never considered television. Like the studio itself, he had not seen the giant potential this new medium presented to his animal. But now, as Maxwell explained it to him, he could visualize Lassie being more successful than the stars of the other old movie concepts that had recently been reused in weekly TV series. When Maxwell offered Rudd and Pal a strong salary plus 10 percent of the profits, the trainer cleared his schedule and began to develop his own ideas about what he felt the show needed.

Maxwell and Rudd came up with the concept of an old-time farm set somewhere in modern-day Middle America. The family would consist of a boy, a mother, and a grandfather. With World War II a recent memory and the Korean War creating a new appreciation for American fighting men, it was decided that the father would have been lost during military service, like Eric Knight himself, thus putting more of a focus on the mother's and grandfather's roles and creating a patriotic stance for the show. Because the family was poor and lacked an active young adult male member, the farm would be a bit run-down, presenting a nostalgic look much like a Norman Rockwell painting. Maxwell knew that even with America becoming more urban, folks still yearned for the ideals of a simpler time.

With this idea in mind, the producer set about putting together a team that could bring it to life. In the middle of this group would be Rudy E. Abel as associate producer. An energetic man, Abel sought out Claire Kennedy, a writer with a homespun touch, to produce a teleplay that would evoke the emotions of the original *Lassie* movie within a rural American setting. Leslie Goodwins, who would later direct episodes of *Tammy* and *Gilligan's Island*, was called in to direct the pilot.

Lassie holds tight to her new mom, Jan Clayton, who had been one of the hottest stars on Broadway before joining Lassie's TV family.

By the time he won the part of George Miller on Lassie, George Cleveland had been acting for more than sixty years.

Jan Clayton, an actress best known for her Broadway performances and quiz-show work, was hired to play the mother, Ellen Miller. Clayton was not that familiar to the general audience, but she was talented, had a good reputation as a hard worker, and seemed very believable in the role. An almost seventy-year-old veteran of more than two hundred films, George Cleveland was hired as the grandfather, George Miller. For Cleveland, a classic character actor, the Lassie pilot meant a reunion with Pal, with whom he had worked on *Courage of Lassie*. All that was left now was to find the boy, Jeff. To do this, the help of another Weatherwax proved crucial.

Rudd's brother, Frank, had been working as the dog trainer on the Dr. Seuss film *The 5,000 Fingers of Dr. T*. The film's juvenile lead had a great résumé and related to the camera very well, but Frank was particularly impressed by the way the youngster worked with animals. As the movie closed production, Weatherwax approached the boy and his mother.

"Frank was training a dog named Mutt for our movie," explained Tom Rettig, "and he came up to me and my mother and told us about his brother putting together a *Lassie* television show. He thought that we might want to contact my agent and have him get in touch with Bob Maxwell. We did, and the next thing I knew I was called in for an interview. At that time I was screen-tested, I read for the part, and evidently I impressed some people. A few weeks later it came down to me and two other kids. One was Lee Aaker, who would eventually star in *Rin Tin Tin*. They decided that all three of us could do the role. So the decision as to who got the part was essentially left up to Lassie."

Rettig, by then eleven, had been acting since his second birthday. While his work had been critiqued by tough talent scouts, costars, and directors, all of them had been human. Not this time. "I spent a week with Rudd and Lassie out in North Hollywood at the Weatherwaxes' home," Tom recalled. "The other finalists did, too. The fact was that Lassie liked me better than he did the other two kids. I loved animals, and this seemed to be very important to Rudd." It must have been important to Lassie, too.

With the cast and crew intact, the two-part pilot's schedule was set up with filming to take place in Calgary. The first story would involve Jeff Miller inheriting Lassie from a neighbor and the bonding of the boy and the dog. The second, featuring a pre–*Leave It to Beaver* Hugh Beaumont, would introduce a typical show to the potential sponsors and network buyers. The fourteen-year-old veteran Pal was called in to be Lassie one more time.

"He didn't seem to be his age," Tom remembered of working with the veteran film dog. "He acted as if he were a puppy. He just loved to perform and work, and he followed Rudd's directions so well that it was easy on all of us. Lassie got more applause than anyone in the cast."

At the end of the first show, the script called for Jeff to turn to Gramps as Lassie charges up to the boy and say, "She's my dog now, isn't she, Gramps?"

Lassie often seemed to have final say on the scripts, although the dog rarely spoke his mind as clearly as did Mr. Ed.

"Yes, boy, she's yours now," Gramps would reply. "She's done her deciding." After viewing that thirty-minute show, CBS quickly did its deciding, too. Lassie would appear on its fall schedule for 1954.

As news of the *Lassie* TV show filtered through the Hollywood publicity machine, MGM's front office got wind of the venture. The studio giant was shocked. They notified their legal office to stop production and draw up a copyright-infringement lawsuit. The studio's latest batch of lawyers contended that they still

owned all rights to the Lassie trademark and name. Before the court action could properly begin, Rudd produced the document showing that some two years before, MGM had given up all rights to Lassie for $40,000. Apparently the junior executives who had cut the deal had failed to inform those at the top. Several of those responsible lost their jobs, but not before MGM lost a potential fortune.

With legal hurdles out of the way, the series set a summer 1954 filming schedule. Scripts were ordered, sets were built, and Lassie found a studio home on Stage One of KTTV in Los Angeles. Pal was as eager as ever to perform, but the dog now called "the Old Man" was not to be a part of this new adventure.

"Really, Pal had had it easy in the movies," Robert Weatherwax explained. "He shot a scene or two a day and then spent the remainder of the time resting. Usually only one movie was made a year. There weren't a whole lot of demands placed on the dog. Television was much more demanding and it called for a much younger dog with much greater endurance. Dad had been working with Lassie, Jr., for a couple of years, and he was three years old and ready. Even though he didn't want to, Dad knew it was time for Pal to give way to his own son."

Now working with the new Lassie, Tom Rettig could sense how hard it was on Pal not to be in front of the camera.

"The Old Man would come to the studio each day, and they had a bed for him just behind the set. When Rudd would ask Lassie, Jr., to do something, if you were behind the set, you could see the Old Man get up from his bed and go through the routine back there."

As Rudd pursued the business of training the new dog and the actors learned their characters, CBS cleared Sunday evening at 7:00 P.M. EST. This was not exactly a great gift on the network's part. Viewership was low at this time and

A page from an early Lassie adventure book, the plots of which closely followed the show's episodes.

Lassie had been taught never to take anything without permission, but this was an emergency. Leaping through the window, she picked up the meat in her mouth, and leaped out again. From the corner of her eye she saw Porky coming into the kitchen.
"Help! Lassie's stealing the roast!" Porky shouted.

the demographic mix was bad. Many people were eating, throughout the Bible Belt people were in church, and televisions usually remained off until 8:00 P.M. The studio really didn't expect much success from any show in this time slot, so it made sense to give it to a new product that only cost $25,000 a week to make. But *Lassie* had found a home, one the show would settle into for some time. Sunday at 7:00 remained *Lassie's* for the next seventeen years, a lengthy run that would be eclipsed by only one other dramatic show—*Gunsmoke*; the only other show to do so well in this period has been *60 Minutes.*

Whitman Publishers introduced a number of Tell-a-Tale books in the fifties featuring Lassie. Lassie and the Kittens was the first of a very successful line.

The popularity and longevity of *Lassie* could not have been predicted, but neither would one have guessed that the network would find a sponsor to carry the whole national commercial load. Campbell's Soups jumped on board early and stayed for the duration. They also took an immediate interest in making sure that *Lassie* portrayed the family values that fit so well with the soup giant's own image. Campbell's didn't have to worry—Bob Maxwell was already making sure that his show fit the all-American image the network and sponsor both wanted.

As Maxwell observed his crew in action he sensed the need for one more piece to make the puzzle complete and ensure the show's success. That extra piece was a seasoned Hollywood director, one who could mold the show into a form that would suit it for years to come. In one of the producer's best moves, he brought in Sheldon Leonard to direct.

As script concepts and the sets were being completed, Rudd took the time to explain to everyone just what was to be expected of Lassie, Jr. First and foremost he didn't want the dog to be a supercanine—he had even turned down a chance for the dog to ap-

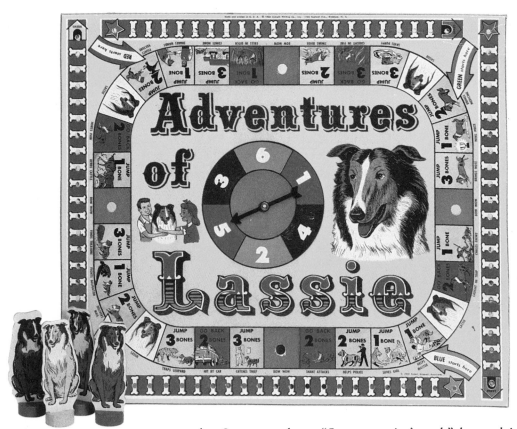

"A wonderful game! Easy to play!" This game was introduced in 1956 with such memorable Lassie adventures inscribed across the board as falls in ditch, caught in fire, saves puppy, traps leopard, and, of course, comes home.

pear on the *Superman* show. "Superman isn't real," he explained, "Lassie is." Therefore Rudd asked those in charge to have Lassie do only normal dog things. The animal was to be the boy's companion, and in that role he would fetch, beg, roll over, and shake. If necessary, he could run for help, fight a villain, or track a lost person. As any dog does from time to time, he could be asked to act jealous, look hurt, and work with other animals. The last was easy. Lassie had been raised around all kinds of creatures and he knew no enemies. He was known to cuddle and play with kittens, chicks, and rabbits, and had even been taught to pick up small bunnies in his mouth. He worked as well with puppies as did female dogs.

Unlike Rudd, the producer didn't put many limits on the writers. They could use any animal they could find, set up a wide variety of calamities, and conjure up storms and floods. Maxwell only requested that each episode teach morals and lessons. The producer felt that television had a responsibility to lead by example, and it was his desire that the Miller family set a positive example.

Campbell's, satisfied that everything else was in order, just asked that their products be placed in grocery sacks and shown in the family's kitchen cabinets. And so in countless episodes of *Lassie*, everything from chicken noodle soup to tomato juice was evident in background shots.

As work began on the first few shows, the production team realized that Jeff needed a friend, someone his own age to react with on a daily basis. Again the casting call went out, and Maxwell invited more than fifteen hundred kids to try out for the part. The number was cut to five hundred, then to fifty, and finally to five. Joey D. Vieira, then known as Donald Keeler, was one of those five.

"They really didn't know what they wanted in the friend," the actor explained. "They didn't know if they wanted short and fat or tall and skinny. So for a week of horrendous auditions we cried, acted, tested, and all tried to be the perfect sidekick. In the end they chose me as Porky."

Porky's network premiere occurred on one of the show's most re-membered episodes, "The Lion." In it, Jeff spots a lion but fails to convince anyone that the beast is on the loose. Finally, alone at the farm, he, Porky, and Lassie come face-to-face with the hungry king of the jungle.

"When you are using lions," Sheldon Leonard re-called, "you don't have any one lion that does every-thing required of him. You bring in a number of lions: one who is peaceful, one who can walk through a scene with-out causing any problems, and another for being vicious. We got these lions from a place in Thou-

A lion named Roger wrecked the kitchen set and got loose in the studio during the filming of an episode called "The Lion."

Porky's Haircut

*V*acationing after the first year of shooting *Lassie* in 1955, Donald Keeler cut his familiar long hair into a buzz style. When he returned to the set, the crew panicked. How was this change of style going to be explained? What would the public think?

Director Bob Maxwell immediately ordered the boy into the dressing room, and a few minutes later none other than Max Factor himself arrived. Factor had long been film's most famous makeup and styling expert. He had worked on Harlow and Monroe, and now he was moving onto his greatest challenge yet, the elegant nine-year-old Porky. Taking out a large suitcase full of supplies, he went to work.

Looking at an old publicity photo of Donald, Factor slowly constructed a wig for the child star. At that same time a group of writers were slapping together a script that could explain why Porky had changed. Within a few hours, Factor had magically transformed an old wig into a Porky hairpiece that looked just as good as the real original. Walking out of the dressing room, wig on head, Keeler was given a new script completely composed in less than two hours. "Learn it," he was told.

Later that day the cast began filming an episode called "The Haircut," in which Keeler (wearing the wig) enters a Calverton barbershop and exits with a buzz cut. For the duration of the series, Donald had orders never again to change his appearance. The first thing he did when he finished his run with *Lassie* was to let his hair grow again.

With the addition of Porky and Pokey, Lassie had six regularly featured players, two of them canines. Thanks to syndication, in many parts of the world this Lassie family is still the best known.

Lassie, Jr., looks proud, if wary, as he and Tom Rettig review the latest crop of Lassie pups.

sand Oaks, and we had a scene where our mean lion was supposed to get into the kitchen as the boys hide under the table.

"To make sure that everything was going to work right and everyone would be safe, we used chicken wire to confine the lion in the area he was supposed to be in. Then the grips built a chute that led from his cage to the kitchen door.

"When they let Roger the tough lion in, he sprang out of his chute, charged into the kitchen, and the first thing he did was look for a way to escape. He smashed the cast-iron stove with one blow of his paw, and then charged the chicken wire that surrounded the set. Chicken wire is great for confining chickens, but it is not much good for holding in a lion."

In a moment of heroism, Lassie, reacting on pure instinct, charged in front of the lion and out the kitchen door. The big cat, whose attention had up until that time been on the two boys, followed the dog. Once off the set, Lassie had no problem getting away from the lion. But having the lion lost in the midst of lights, sound equipment, portable dressing rooms, and scores of unsuspecting people was a problem for everyone else.

"A television set is a very cluttered thing," Leonard explained. "Things are stacked and piled up everywhere. It's like a maze to walk through, and in this maze we couldn't see the lion. We didn't know where Roger was or where he was going.

"At the end of the building was an exit right out onto Sunset Boulevard. I could just imagine what would happen if the lion were to get loose out on the street, and so I yelled at Jack Weatherwax, Rudd's seventeen-year-old son, to run down and block the door to the outside."

As Leonard and the crew watched the teenager race toward the door, they suddenly saw Roger trying to beat him there. Jack arrived just in time to turn and be greeted by the huge beast. The lion's trainer yelled out, "Don't move and he won't bother you," so Jack stood perfectly still as the lion sniffed and resniffed every part of his body. Finally, after what seemed like an eternity to Jack and the crew, the trainer got the beast back in the chute and the crew started to come out of their hiding places.

"We all made a hero out of young Weatherwax," Leonard laughed. "I said to him, 'My God, it was brave of you to stand so still with that lion sniffing all around you.'

"Weatherwax looked back at me and said, 'Sir, at that time that lion had a great deal to sniff. Now may I go change my clothes?'"

While having lions loose on the set was not the norm, elephants, chimps, and raccoons created problems every time they were used. Simply surviving this kind of work may have helped make Sheldon Leonard one of the real legends of television.

"From my weeks on the *Lassie* show I learned to be flexible and improvise," the director acknowledged. "When you worked with animals, you had to. I took that with me wherever I worked in the future."

Shooting *Lassie* was tough on everyone. Because they were filming fifteen pages a day, six

One of the things Porky couldn't seem to get enough of was Ellen's cooking, although Jan Clayton, of course, never really cooked a crumb.

Lassie, Jr., traveled in haute-fifties style, riding in a fancy air-conditioned Chrysler station wagon of his own.

days a week, and three complete shows each week, they didn't have the luxury of shooting in order. The crew might shoot three or four straight barn segments and then move to the kitchen to do the same. These shots would then be used in four or five different shows. It was a grind, but it was made easier by the congenial atmosphere on the set.

"It may have had to do with the early days of television," Rettig noted, "but we were very much a family. Jan Clayton was a second mom to me, and Rudd was like the father I didn't have. I think we were all so comfortable because the characters we were playing were very much like we really were. George Cleveland was very much like Gramps. Donald and I were a great deal like Porky and Jeff. It was a warm and comfortable place."

Lassie, Jr., his father's look-alike, was enjoying his days on the set, too. He immediately bonded with young Rettig, and from the first day of filming the two spent a great deal of time together. Often Tom would go home on the weekends with Rudd and play with Lassie and Rudd's youngest son, Robert. With Rudd's encouragement, Tom began brushing Lassie every morning, and at lunch break the dog and boy would spend the entire hour together.

Initially, having the boy and dog grow so close seemed perfect. It made the scenes they did together much easier to film, for the cameras caught the true devotion that the dog felt for the boy. But after a few months a problem developed that began to undermine scene after scene—Lassie developed a split loyalty and began to question who was his master. When Rudd would call him, rather than react immediately the dog would often look at Tom to make sure that he was doing the right thing. Even though he didn't like to do it, Rudd was forced to separate Tom and Lassie when they weren't shooting.

This Is Your Life!

Lassie's celebrity knew no bounds, and at its height the dog appeared on a spoof of *This Is Your Life* with Bob Hope. Ordinarily unflappable, Hope found himself cackling, laughing, and finally collapsing in hysteria as he introduced the dogs in Lassie's life. Beginning with the story of the star's puppyhood ("Your mother was a retired sheepdog and your father, well, he was a gay dog..."), Hope brought in Lassie's best friend, first great love, and a series of other purported acquaintances played by highly trained trick dogs who walked on their hind legs and were outfitted as jazz musicians, babies in carriages, horses ridden by cowboys, professional boxers, and elegant gentlemen. As the audience howled and Lassie looked on calmly, her film career was reviewed ("Your first role was a small part in *The Canine Mutiny*..."), she was presented with gifts for appearing on the show (six mambo lessons and a do-it-yourself rabies kit), and Hope signed off: "Yours has been a dog's life," he cheered, "and so we say, This Is Your Life, Lassie!"

From day one *Lassie* was a hit, and even during that first season the awards and recognition came rolling in at a steady pace. In 1955, Tom Rettig and Donald Keeler accepted the Emmy for Best Children's Program. That same year the show also pulled down a host of other awards, including top honors from the PTA, the Gold Star, the National Association for Better Radio and Television, and *Billboard.* Adventure Books, Golden Books, coloring books, puzzles, Halloween costumes, and many other items hit the marketplace. Fan letters to the tune of two thousand a week poured in for the dog, and another three thousand a week were addressed to members of the cast. Lassie now commanded $2,000 for a standard personal appearance, and Bob Hope paid him $2,500 for one appearance on a *This Is Your Life* takeoff that would have Hope in convulsions.

Both Lassie, Jr., and Pal appeared on the September 26, 1954, cover of *Parade,* and over the next few years the dog would grace *Life, Look,* and earn three *TV Guide* covers as well. On an average week thirty-three million viewers tuned in, and over a period of one year the network sent out more than forty thousand pawtographed photos.

Vice President Richard M. Nixon congratulates Tom Rettig for his work on behalf of the Treasury's Saving Stamps Drive.

Lassie now traveled via commercial jetliner and first-class only. The cars he rode in were all air-conditioned. He stayed in the very nicest hotels, slept in double beds, had his own pet dog to play with, and ate only the best food—homemade beef stews or occasional lean cuts of steak. He even had a fan-club and a fan-club scrapbook that thousands of kids treasured. He was the biggest canine star ever, and one of the biggest stars in the entertainment business.

6 FIRST PRIZES
plus
625 OTHER BIG PRIZES
See schedule on reverse side

FRANCO-AMERICAN CONTEST

WIN $2,000 and a "LASSIE" PUPPY

Fill out and mail to: LASSIE, P.O. Box 70-C, Mt. Vernon 10, N.Y.

HERE IS MY NAME FOR A "LASSIE" PUPPY—

I am enclosing <u>two</u> Franco-American labels

Name...
(Please Print)

Address...

State.............

Campbell's Soup ran a contest in 1956 to help name Lassie's puppies, the winners of which received one of the pups and $2,000. Seven-year-old Judy Czerminski of Rochester, New York (right) grins happily with her new pet Lassie puppy, won in the contest.

In 1956 any trick-or-treater could purchase a Lassie costume for Halloween. This odd Lassie collectible is now very rare and highly sought after.

To his sponsor, this popularity was clearly reflected in the growth of their soup sales as well as responses to their special Lassie offers. In 1956 Campbell's offered a free Lassie photo to anyone who would send in two chicken-soup labels. This ploy received 35,935 replies—a lot of noodles. Because of their great impact, Lassie and his cast members were now considered the soup company's marketing teammates. The whole cast began doing commercials for different kinds of soup, appearing in company-sponsored public-service spots for savings stamps, and traveling the nation on behalf of their sponsor. For all practical purposes, Campbell's was Lassie's middle name, and the soup company wanted everyone to know it.

One of their more successful Campbell's promotions involved a contest to name Lassie's puppies, each winner receiving one of the nippers. In response to a show on which Lassie gave birth (quite a trick for a male dog), hundreds of thousands of suggestions were mailed into the company. A blue-ribbon committee chose the winners and then company executives flew to the winners' homes and delivered the collie pups in person.

Many press reports were now predicting that Lassie could go on forever. With profits mounting and the popularity of the show's human stars on a par with that of any motion-picture idol, it seemed that he just might.

Still, Bob Maxwell wasn't so sure. By the third season all the original plots were just about used up, the farm setting seemed to have its limits, and the show's main human star was beginning to create some problems: There was nothing wrong with Tom Rettig's acting or personality, but he *was* growing up. As Maxwell told several people, "Boys grow up, dogs don't. We have a problem because Tom is getting older. With that in mind the format isn't going to work too much longer. A teenager and his dog doesn't make much sense."

In many ways he was right. The show had already used more wild animals than Tarzan. Lassie had saved Jeff's life in more ways than anyone could remember. The dog had survived shootings and poisonings, had given birth to a couple of litters of puppies, and had been falsely accused (and acquitted) of countless despicable acts, including killing and eating sheep. Near the Miller farm Jeff and Porky had been caught in caves and swamps, on mountain ledges and river bottoms. What more could be done? Besides, Tom was now picking out a car to buy, going out on dates, and thinking about college. All these things seemed to point to the end of the road, so the producer quietly put the show on the market.

Maxwell quickly found a buyer in Texas oilman Jack Wrather,

Where Are They Now?

TOM RETTIG: After acting off and on through the late seventies, he became a highly successful creator of computer software programs. Based in northern California, he has earned a long list of credits, including work on the design of Ashton-Tate's dBASE software. Since establishing his own company in 1985, he has won numerous awards for his products, including Tom Rettig's Library and Tom Rettig's HELP. In fact he is now much more famous as a computer-program developer than as an actor, which suits him just fine.

DONALD KEELER: Using his real name, Joey D. Vieira, the ex-Porky has continued his acting career. Most recently he was seen in *Red Heat, Ferris Bueller's Day Off*, and *Pray for Us All.* The father of two grown children, he has appeared on scores of television shows since leaving *Lassie.* He lives just over a hill outside Los Angeles where most of *Lassie's* outdoor lake footage was shot.

JAN CLAYTON: When she completed her work on *Lassie,* Clayton acted on Broadway and television for many years. After successfully battling alcoholism, she also worked with Alcoholics Anonymous as a spokesperson. She and Tom Rettig remained close until her death in 1983.

Bonita Granville Wrather being wished a happy Mother's Day by her show's star.

who was married to actress Bonita Granville. While the former child movie star was no longer actively pursuing her film career, she wanted to keep her hands in show business. By purchasing *Lassie* (Wrather already owned *The Lone Ranger* and *Sergeant Preston of the Yukon*), the multimillionaire could give his wife something that would satisfy her creative needs. He also felt that this was a wise business move. Wrather knew that Lassie could be marketed more appropriately. The oilman sensed that the show was still heading up, and he believed all it needed was some fine-tuning.

Wrather offered Maxwell $3.25 million for all rights to the dog show, about a dime for every one of Lassie's individual viewers. In the agreement Weatherwax was to be retained for his standard contract and a percentage—adding up to $100,000 a year—and Lassie would earn $1,500 a week. Finally, Maxwell would have to stay on for one additional year as executive producer in order to make sure that the show went through a smooth transition of ownership. Wrather was convinced that he had made the deal of a lifetime. So was a smiling Maxwell.

Rudd, a bit uneasy over the change, took some of his money and purchased a new ranch. If things didn't work out, he would have a nice place to call home. When *TV Guide* asked him about buying the new property, he laughed, "Lassie bought it. Let's face it, Lassie buys everything."

But for once Lassie couldn't buy happiness, as the original cast discovered during its last year together. Tom Rettig was tired of not being able to go anywhere without being recognized. "I

Faux Lassie

During the television era, much was made of exactly how many dogs it took to film an episode of *Lassie*. Rudd Weatherwax took great pains to explain that there was only one Lassie, and that the star did about 95 percent of the work on each show. Other dogs were used only as stand-ins for setting up shots, he explained, or for long shots if Lassie had been working very hard in an earlier scene.

The dog that was used most often as the double was Laddie, Lassie, Jr.'s, brother and Pal's son. All but identical to the star, complete with blaze and full white collar, Laddie would sometimes fill in during shots that would have messed up Lassie's coat, such as those that involved rolling in the mud or swimming. Since Lassie, Jr., was written into almost every scene of every show, if he got muddy the crew would be forced to wait until he could be regroomed for the next shot. So Laddie's work as a stand-in allowed the crew to keep to a tight schedule.

Lassie, Jr., clears a hurdle just after his brother Laddie, a dog used as both a stand-in and stunt double. Though not nearly as beautiful as his brother, Laddie was equally talented and was used in a number of the fight scenes.

couldn't go in the main door of a theater to watch a movie," he remembered. "I couldn't go to public school. I always had people asking me where my collie was. I couldn't escape being Jeff Miller." Now a teenager, the actor was growing up and wanted to move on.

Jan Clayton was tired, too. She missed Broadway, and she was also having to cope with the tragic death of her teenage daughter in a car wreck. Originally she had signed a four-year contract and she vowed to stick to it, but she didn't want to take on any more than that. She really needed a change of pace.

George Cleveland had the opposite problem—he wanted to stay on, but he realized that he would have to live with the decisions that best suited Rettig, Clayton, and the show. Donald Keeler didn't want to leave either. He liked the work and he was getting more fan mail than anyone besides Lassie. "The ugly girls liked me," he laughed when explaining his popularity.

Meanwhile, Lassie, Jr., just went about his business as usual. He ran into burning barns, fought wolves, rescued children, played nursemaid to a hundred different animals, faked injuries, and raised puppies. He was the star, and how to keep him at the top was inspiring endless debates among the new owners, the producers, and the sponsors.

Campbell's, the Wrathers, Rudd Weatherwax, and Bob Maxwell worked and discussed the problem for months as *Lassie* ran on smoothly. As the players' contracts ran out and as the beginning of a fourth season crept up, the team finally decided to phase the existing family out in a gentle way, find a new boy, and, over a three-show period, bring this lad and Lassie to the forefront. It sounded easy and it probably could have been, but accomplishing this transformation proved to be a monumental challenge.

Trouble in Paradise:
A Show in Transition

*I*n the spring of 1957 it became apparent that Bob Maxwell and the Wrathers had yet to come up with a way to remodel *Lassie* without taking the chance of destroying the product and losing the devotion of over thirty million viewers. The start of filming for the fourth season was just a few weeks off, and even though they had interviewed more than two hundred boys, they still hadn't found one they thought could play the pivotal role, nor had they come up with a way to introduce him into the cast.

Campbell's Soup officials had requested that the present cast stay intact as much as possible. In a letter to Jack Wrather they stated, "We believe that if we lose all three stars we're going to be up the creek with that valuable dog. We don't mind if you give us a transition, but don't allow this to become an upheaval." Their concern proved justified.

Before anything could really be done, they had to find a way to ease another boy onto the show, as well as to slowly allow Rettig, who was now old enough to drive a car, to withdraw. It now seemed unfortunate that Bob Maxwell had not given Jeff Miller a little brother when he and Rudd Weatherwax had created the pilot.

The first bit of hopeful news concerning the transition came from Bonita Granville Wrather, who had found a child she thought could be the next little boy. He was only six, but he had appeared in more than a dozen movies over the past four years, and she assured them all that he was "precious." The camera and the audience would love him.

Jon Provost and his mother didn't know that the Wrathers were looking for a new boy for *Lassie*. If they had, they might have come to one of the early casting calls. Instead, they had temporarily left for the Orient, where Jon was on location, filming *Escapade in Japan* for RKO. Back in the States, the wife of *Escapade*'s producer was eating lunch one day with Bonita Granville Wrather, who mentioned their lack of success in finding a boy to play on *Lassie*. The producer's wife told Bonita about Jon, with whom they had just worked, and when the boy came back to the country he met with the *Lassie* producers. After one meeting he got the job—but on a provisional basis. He could really only claim to be Lassie's new

Previous page: Jeff and Ellen bid farewell to a mournful Timmy and Porky, leaving Lassie with Ruth and Paul Martin. This would be the last time Tom Rettig would ever work on the CBS Lassie, although Jan Clayton and Donald Keeler would return for one final episode.

master after spending a week on Rudd's ranch to see how he and the dog got along. In a matter of just three days Jon got Lassie's approval.

Now that they had the little boy with a salary of $350 a week, the producers and writers had to figure a way to work him into the show. After much debate they finally decided to open the season with a script called "The Runaway." In the show, Jon played a young child who has run away from his aged guardians in order to make life easier on them. Lassie discovers him in the Miller barn and before the twenty-two minutes had finished and the last commercial had run, Ellen Miller convinces his guardians and the child welfare agency to allow "Timmy" to spend the summer on the Miller farm. Everyone agreed as they watched the rushes that their plan had worked beautifully. Timmy was perfect for the show.

Lassie, Jr., was the only dog to work with both Tom Rettig and Jon Provost as well as all three of the Lassie moms, Jan Clayton, Cloris Leachman, and June Lockhart.

In one of the show's lesser-known bits of historical trivia, the name Timmy was chosen because that was the name of Bonita Granville's mother. Finding Jon and choosing his character's name were the ex-actress's first moves in getting heavily involved with the show. As the years went by, she would exert more and more creative control.

Rudd Weatherwax also felt good about both Provost and his character, yet he worried that as young as Jon was, there might be some problems in keeping him from accidentally mistreating Lassie. With that in mind, he approached the boy and his mother with an offer.

"Rudd made a deal with me," Jon remembered. "If I didn't ride, kick, sit on, or bother Lassie, then he would give me a puppy at the end of the first year. To me, this sounded great. All I had to

do was behave and I could have what every boy who had grown up watching the show wanted—one of Lassie's pups."

With Timmy entrenched in the series and everyone so happy with Jon, most people expected the transition from one cast to another to move quickly and smoothly. "We thought that it would all take place over a three-show story line," Tom Rettig recalled. "Yet three shows came and went, and then three more came and went, and there was no hint of a transition. The writers just seemed to be accepting Timmy into the old format and otherwise leaving well enough alone." Rettig's suspicions were on target. While in many ways Timmy had become a central character, and he was spending a great deal of time with Lassie in front of the camera, *Lassie* was very much the same show it had always been. The producers and writers simply used Jon with Lassie instead of Tom—it was easier and more practical than creating a new show.

With the fall premiere so close, things couldn't have seemed better. The producers could now be completely satisfied that with

Campbell's used both the dog and the cast to help them sell soup, a practice that had begun with Jan Clayton, Tom Rettig, and Donald Keeler. By the time June Lockhart and Jon Provost were introduced, the soup giant considered Lassie and company a part of the corporate team.

MY TEN DAYS IN RUSSIA
SEE PAGE 1

Campbell People

CAMPBELL SOUP COMPANY

NOVEMBER 1957   CAMDEN EDITION

the simple move of adding one child they had accomplished what the show needed. As the new season unfolded it seemed to prove them right, for with each new episode viewership was climbing. Adding Timmy had given the series a new story line and had allowed Jan Clayton and George Cleveland to expand their characters. The sponsor was happy because the show was selling more soup than ever. With things going so well, the thinking was that Maxwell and Wrather might be able to get Rettig and Clayton to change their minds about not renewing their contracts and could then rewrite the scripts in such a way that would make them both happy enough to stay on with the show.

But the first real problem with keeping the Miller family intact arose when

Maxwell discovered that no state allowed an unmarried mother to adopt an unrelated child. Hence, Ellen couldn't go to court and really become Timmy's mom. With this option out, the producers considered marriage and then adoption. Clayton was against it. She wanted to go back to her work in musicals, and besides, who would they introduce as her love interest? The concept was just too complicated to set into motion in the time frame that they had. So as show powers huddled and debated possible scenarios, the writers continued to stall by creating more "normal" shows involving elephants, chimps, and heroic rescues. Then real tragedy struck, and the Wrathers and Maxwell had no choice but to make a major move.

As Jon Provost's star continued to rise, a highly successful line of Timmy and Lassie clothing was introduced. Few examples of the collie-festooned outfits survive.

"No one planned on George Cleveland having a heart attack and dying," Tom Rettig explained. "It was all very sudden and unexpected."

Cleveland's death put the set into a near panic. For several weeks production shut down. There was no logical way to write Cleveland out of the show now. Some suggested that he break a hip and be shipped off to a distant hospital, but that didn't hold with the family's closeness. Finally, Maxwell took matters into his own hands and decided to face the issue head-on by simply telling the viewers the truth. Gramps had died.

The writers pasted together a quick story that begins at the house just after George Miller's funeral. From there Timmy overhears Ellen and Jeff talking about the fact that the child welfare bureau will probably now have to take the small boy away from them. Without a man on the place, the family

Lassie may not have paid taxes but the dog made enough money for the show's owners and sponsors to pay a great deal.

will also have to sell the farm. When a young couple, Ruth and Paul Martin, comes to visit and discuss the possibility of purchasing the farm, Timmy runs away thinking he is going to be sent back to his relatives. With Lassie's help, Paul Martin finds him and saves the boy from drowning. By the end of the show, the Millers have packed, the Martins have adopted Timmy, and Jeff has given Lassie to the younger boy. It had taken thirteen episodes, but on the first Sunday night in December 1957, the transition was finally complete and the special show aired.

Ideally that would have been it, but even from the start it was obvious to both viewers and the producers that there were problems. Cloris Leachman, a former beauty contestant with a great deal of Broadway and television experience, had been quickly hired to play Ruth Martin. Jon Shepodd, a man with a limited acting background known mainly for his comic skills, was chosen to play Paul. Shepodd worked pretty well and the viewers seemed to feel immediately positive about his character. On the other hand Leachman just didn't fit in, and from the start the *Lassie* fans and some of the crew didn't like her.

"I adored Jan Clayton," dialogue coach Lloyd Nelson recalled. "She was wonderful, a real neighbor, a real friend. Cloris was a good person and funny, but compared to Jan it was a total change of pace when she came in. She would roll in for work in the morning in these hot-purple pedal pushers, and in all honesty she had a body that wouldn't quit. She would sashay through the set looking that way, and then come out of makeup and hair looking like Ruth Martin."

It was quickly apparent to most on the set that Cloris was used to being the lead, and it must have been very evident to her that in *Lassie* she wasn't. The dog and the child got the close-ups, while the mother simply played the supporting role. Plus, dressing and acting like a tired farm woman did not appear to suit her image.

On the other side of the screen, many viewers who had grown to love the empathic and sincere Ellen Miller were put off

In one particularly strange episode, Jimmy's dream transports him to a nightmare land where Jeff is the dog warden and Jimmy must pick out which Lassie is his own.

In 1958 Lassie got a new family: Jon Shepodd, Cloris Leachman, and Jon Provost. Less than six months after this happy shot was taken, only Provost and Lassie were still with the series.

by Cloris's Ruth Martin. She was too stiff, too cold, and seemed out of place on a farm.

"She had a contract for thirty-nine shows," Lloyd Nelson remembered, "and she would never sign the contract. The entire time she was on the show, she refused to sign the thing. And what was worse, she wasn't the least bit interested in doing any P.R. for the show or the sponsor. She told Campbell's that she wouldn't do publicity for them because, she said, 'I make my own soup, I don't eat yours.' That didn't go over too well."

Within a few shows, Wrather had seen enough. He had to do something to make *Lassie* a warm and happy place to spend a Sunday night again, but it had to be a quick fix that wouldn't disturb what had already been done. A casting call was sent out for an old man to come in as Paul's uncle. Maybe a grandfatherly type like

George Cleveland had played could regenerate some of the positive feelings the first cast had so naturally exhibited.

George Chandler, a movie character actor who had only recently turned to television, was hired for the part. In the story line it was explained that Uncle Petrie was needed to help Paul run the farm. Proving what a great guy he was, in his debut Chandler played the guitar, told stories and jokes, and even made a Lassie ring for Timmy to wear. To exploit the plot and the publicity created by Chandler's arrival, Campbell's offered copies of the ring to anyone who would mail in twenty-five cents and a label from one of their Swanson's frozen dinners. Before the promotion ended the soup giant had mailed out 77,715 rings.

While he might have been able to sell jewelry, Uncle Petrie wasn't able to affect the show's downward roll. Part of the problem with Petrie's acceptance was the explanation offered for the uncle's arrival. For all those years Gramps and Ellen had managed to work the farm just fine all by themselves, and Gramps had been old. Why couldn't this supposedly vibrant young couple do the work themselves, too? Were they inept, were they just lazy, or had they overextended their budget? After all, there was a new pickup and a new car sitting out in the driveway. For three seasons there had been very few reasons to dislike *Lassie;* now that number in-

For the first half of the transition season, things stayed much as they had, although now Lassie worked with Timmy almost as much as Jeff.

Lassie, Jr., takes a call informing him that he and his new master are doing a great job and that help in the form of new parents is on the way.

Nothing was too good for television star Lassie, Jr. Silver bowls, monogrammed blankets, and linen tablecloths were standard fare, even at the famous Los Angeles restaurant Chasens.

creased with each episode.

Things on the set grew more tense with each passing week, and the behind-the-scenes feuds were making television gossip columns. The fact was that Leachman and Chandler did not like each other, and from time to time they let it show. Shepodd, still fairly wet behind his acting ears, usually faded back into the shadows rather than come between either of his more experienced costars. Directors and writers were going crazy. Working with this group made working with animals look easy. All the adults, but especially Cloris, wanted more time on camera, which meant less time for Lassie. The only saving grace was that the public was falling in love with Jon Provost, and so the story lines centered more and more on him and the dog. This was not lost on the others.

Lassie and the Stork

Whenever Lassie traveled he received a multitude of invitations to social functions. A sophisticated dog, he was as much at home at the White House as he was on the farm, and he was so well trained that most leash laws were waived just for his sake.

One of the dog's more elegant soirées came in December 1957, while Lassie, Jr., was appearing as the star attraction at New York's Madison Square Garden Rodeo. After the show Rudd Weatherwax changed into evening wear, Lassie ran a brush through his coat, and the two stepped out to the city's famous Stork Club.

With hundreds looking on, Rudd and Lassie strolled into the Stork and asked for a corner table close to the stage. And although the big collie had neglected to wear a tie, he was photographed avidly for the society pages.

Things look like they couldn't be happier in this howl-along publicity shot. But behind the scenes, Cloris Leachman and George Chandler did not get along at all, and the set was often chilled with hostility.

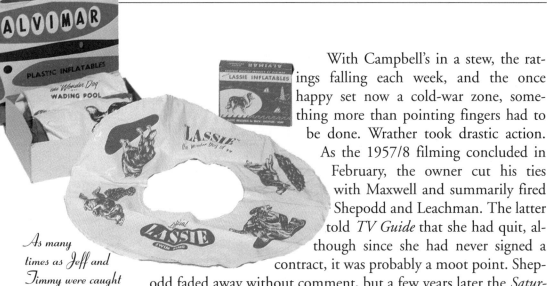

As many times as Jeff and Timmy were caught in raging rivers, they could have used this inflatable Lassie swim ring. In the box is "the Wonder Dog's" wading pool.

With Campbell's in a stew, the ratings falling each week, and the once happy set now a cold-war zone, something more than pointing fingers had to be done. Wrather took drastic action. As the 1957/8 filming concluded in February, the owner cut his ties with Maxwell and summarily fired Shepodd and Leachman. The latter told *TV Guide* that she had quit, although since she had never signed a contract, it was probably a moot point. Shepodd faded away without comment, but a few years later the *Saturday Evening Post* got Cloris to talk about her experience. She laughingly replied, "They had to find reasons for us to be morons so the dog could outsmart us. I can't say I miss the dog, we were never that close." Lassie never seemed to miss Cloris either.

The least offensive episodes of the last year were chosen for the summer rerun season and the Rettig years were sold into syndication as *Jeff's Collie.* The latter would be broadcast around the world for years in dozens of languages and make Rettig, Clayton, Cleveland, and Keeler familiar faces to new generations.

With the nasty business behind them but still facing an uphill battle to save their million-dollar investment, Wrather and his wife

Originally made for Timmy by Uncle Petrie, the Lassie friendship ring was copied and offered to Campbell's customers.

Get a **LASSIE FRIENDSHIP RING!**
ONLY **25¢** and a label from **SWANSON**
MEAT PIES or "TV" BRAND DINNERS
EXTRA! A wallet size color picture of Lassie and Timmy included with each Friendship Ring.
USE ORDER FORM ON REVERSE SIDE

LASSIE FRIENDSHIP RING
★ 20 Karat Gold Plated Band
★ Sterling Silver Sculptured Lassie Inset
★ Adjustable to fit any size finger

began a search for a new producer and a new on-screen couple who could restore warmth to the familiar old farm and their television show. For the former post Jack Wrather had called upon the skills of his old friend Bob Golden, an experienced producer who could manage the daily problems of shooting a series. Plus he knew everybody in the business and would be a great help in finding a new set of parents.

Golden quickly realized that Lassie was more than just a TV show. To many, including Rudd, this show and this dog were almost a sacred trust. When Bob Maxwell had hurriedly changed the cast, he had not realized this. Golden did. "If we were going to fool with *Lassie*, we had better do it right or we were going to hear about it. It wasn't like doing another show."

Jon and Lassie, Jr., kept things afloat while the cast and crew struggled to define what the Wrather-owned version of the show would become.

When the Miller family left the farm and the Martins moved in, Lassie's credits received a makeover, including new theme music, a new opening, and the addition of the famous "whistling" ending.

So with a great deal of care, hoping to choose someone whom they and the public would grow to love, Bonita Granville Wrather and Bob Golden looked through résumés and film clips for a new Ruth and Paul Martin.

Ultimately, they found the father on a Broadway stage. Hugh Reilly had been a success in Broadway comedies and in dramatic television shows. While his face was not well known, he was respected for his acting as well as for his ability to get along with cast and crew.

Finding Hugh had involved a great deal of effort. But discovering the person who would play the new and improved Ruth Martin was as easy as driving down Sunset Boulevard and pulling up beside a beautiful woman at a stop sign.

When George Cleveland had died, before Bob Maxwell signed Cloris Leachman, Maxwell and the Wrathers had spoken with June Lockhart. They had even offered the actress a chance to step in and try out for the part. At the time June was living in New York and she didn't want to relocate to Los Angeles. She turned them down without as much as a second thought. Eight months later, though, she had moved back to California and was working on both coasts, flying to jobs and very aware of how much she missed her two young daughters when she was away.

One spring day, Bonita Wrather and Bob Golden pulled up to a Hollywood stop sign and found their car side by side with Lockhart's.

"I remember exchanging greetings," Bob recalled, "and then I

The Wonderful World of Lassie— seven of twelve Lassie coloring books from the late fifties.

Campbell's

LASSIE & TIMMY PICTURE ON THIS LABEL

PORK & BEANS

WITH TOMATO SAUCE

DIRECTIONS
Place the contents of this can in a saucepan or casserole, heat and serve.

NET WEIGHT 1 POUND

MADE BY
CAMPBELL SOUP COMPANY
GENERAL OFFICES, CAMDEN, N. J. U.S.A.
REG. U.S. PAT. OFF.

Campbell's PORK & BEANS

TIMMY—LASSIE'S PAL

STARS OF THE "LASSIE" TV SHOW

When Lassie and Timmy appeared on the can, sales of Campbell's Pork & Beans skyrocketed.

asked her, 'How would you like to be Lassie's mom?'" June laughed and replied, "Yes, sure, but only for about a year."

Shaking her head, Bonita sighed and said, "I'm sorry, that is just not long enough," then watched as June waved good-bye and drove off.

"As I drove home I thought about what I had been offered," Lockhart would remember, "and I said to myself, 'What am I being so damn grand about? I have two children to support, the part they want me to play has a lot of dignity, the show is already on the air, I wouldn't have to film a pilot, and they have a sponsor. This is really a great gift that has been offered me. I'd be stupid not to at least look into it.'"

It was ironic that Bonita and Bob were interested in June Lockhart to play the all-American farm woman, since a little more than a decade before she had won a movie role in *Son of Lassie* because she had seemed so British.

With the new cast complete and the Wrathers assured that this group would offer them no problems, it was time to put together a season in which Lassie and the viewer would have a warm place to call home. On that first day with Hugh Reilly and June Lockhart on the set, it was obvious to the owners that their risky move had worked magic.

As the summer rolled along and the new episodes began to be

Ho Ho Ho Indeed

Campbell's had a huge commitment to Lassie, and the company's investment was well repaid. With *Lassie*'s success fueling Campbell's, the food giant's sales skyrocketed. Kids bugged their moms to purchase whatever it was that Jeff, Porky, or Timmy was eating. Mothers also seemed to trust Ellen and Ruth when they appeared in commercials for Campbell's. In addition, the cast did public relations work for the company and agreed for its sake not to make appearances in anything that would undermine the show's all-American image. But was Campbell's grateful?

In a way. Every year at Christmas, the *Lassie* cast received a unique bonus from their sponsor—wicker baskets filled with dented cans of the company's soup. June Lockhart recalled that eventually the baskets were replaced by plain sacks. "And they never gave us the good kinds," Donald Keeler added. "It was always the stuff that they couldn't sell even if the cans hadn't been dented."

Merry Christmas from Ruth, Timmy and Lassie.

Originally June Lockhart had turned down a chance to replace Jan Clayton, thus opening the door for Cloris Leachman. When Leachman left the show, the good-humored Lockhart stepped in and is credited with stabilizing a floundering series.

completed, the set once again lit up and the Wrathers began to re-lax. Their $3 million plus investment seemed to be about to pay off. Their first year on the show they may have stumbled out the gate, but now things were different. Still, it would be the viewers who would decide if this overhaul had happened soon enough, and that verdict would have to wait until September.

The Timmy Years:
A Dog and His Boy

"The Storm," episode 5805, kicked off the 1958/9 season. According to the straightforward script, Timmy and his friend Boomer attempt to teach Boomer's dog, Mike, some tricks. The dog can't learn until Lassie shows the boys that Mike is deaf. The boys then get Doc Weaver to fix Mike's hearing and he becomes a great farm dog. Thrown into this mix is a subplot about a cyclone in which Lassie risks his life to save Mike. To the millions of viewers who tuned in for the fall premiere, the action and plot seemed perfectly normal; the only thing different was Timmy's parents.

"One Sunday evening my parents were Cloris Leachman and Jon Shepodd," Jon Provost recalled about that September 1958 premiere, "and the next Sunday they were the same parents, only this time played by June Lockhart and Hugh Reilly. There was not a bit of explanation." And none was needed. As they had accepted Timmy Martin, Americans embraced Lockhart and Reilly without question. The kid and the dog were the same, and to the viewers that seemed to be all that mattered. At the time, that was about all that mattered to Provost also.

"When Cloris and Jon left and were replaced by June and Hugh," Jon explained, "it really didn't make too much difference to me. I wasn't close to either Cloris or Jon, and all I cared about was the dog. Honestly, at that time the parents didn't enter into the picture." Still, it wouldn't take long for him to feel differently.

"When June Lockhart came in," remembered Lloyd Nelson, "I was in love again. Just like Jan Clayton, June was wonderful. I felt then, and I still feel, that when June left the show six years later, the whole thing went downhill. In my mind the best *Lassie* was when the show had Lockhart, Reilly, and Provost." Ratings, lasting appeal, and soup sales seemed to agree with the script consultant.

Lassie was once again wildly popular with the audience. The show consistently placed in the top twenty, and it would be this show, this cast, and this format that would be etched most clearly in the minds of the country's baby boomers. The critics would long point to the first three years of *Lassie* as being the best written, directed, and acted, and two Emmys seemed to prove this assessment. But now there were millions more television sets, tens of

Previous page: This chimp looked friendly enough during filming, but he almost took Jon's thumb off when the shooting finished.

millions more people in front of them, and opportunities for almost limitless access to those viewers. Television was no longer a new toy, it was big business, and no one seemed to know more about making money in this business than Jack Wrather.

Satisfied with the new core cast, the oilman and his wife began to fine-tune the show. One of the first things they did was to take a look at Timmy's relationship with other cast members.

When Shepodd and Leachman had gotten the ax, George Chandler had hung on as Uncle Petrie, but with the viewers' overwhelming acceptance of Lockhart and Reilly, Chandler's part was quickly diminished. He had been brought in only to help ease and soften Cloris Leachman's negative image, and it was thought that he could be to the Martin family what Gramps had been to the Millers. Unfortunately not even a seasoned veteran like Chandler could stack up next to George Cleveland's characterization of the grouchy but good-hearted Gramps. As the popularity of Lockhart and Reilly grew, the need for an uncle ceased to exist. Finally, saying that the father needed more contact with Timmy, the producers eased Chandler out of the show altogether.

Todd Ferrell had

Happy New Year from Lassie and the cast of television's most popular family show.

Boomer, his dog Mike, Jon, and Lassie, Jr., share the bench in front of the barn set.

been hired to play Timmy's best friend, Boomer, during the troubled transition year. Todd was cute and an adequate actor, yet the role of Boomer never took off as had been expected, and Todd Ferrell did not elicit the popular response of Keeler's Porky. By the middle of the next season, he too, like Chandler, was written out. With Lassie, Timmy, Ruth, and Paul, little else was needed.

Lassie, Jr., a dog who was Rudd's pride and joy, was happy no matter who was in the cast. Like his father, he lived for the action, he enjoyed showing off, and he loved attention. Also, much like his father, he was a one-owner dog. Except for his initial relationship with Tom Rettig, this Lassie only had eyes for Rudd. The dog felt little attachment to anyone else, which was the way it had to be. While Jon Provost did get to play with Lassie, the dog who was this boy's best friend was back at home. In exchange for good behavior the previous year, Jon had indeed been given one of Lassie's pups, and he had named it Rudd.

In the midst of Wrather's fine-tuning, one thing didn't change, and that was the scripts. To a large degree the plots for this version of

Lassie were very much like those of the show's first three years. The boy would get in some kind of trouble, usually with a wild or misunderstood animal. Lassie, who always seemed to sense that this had not been a good idea from the start, would then either save her owner's life himself or get help in time. Then, after Timmy had been embraced by Ruth and Paul and everyone breathed a deep sigh of relief, the boy would receive a light lecture on why he shouldn't have done what he had done. With the small moral lesson successfully taught, everyone was happy and the final credits would roll. As simple and sometimes as bland as it seemed, this formula was perfect, and it kept *Lassie* far and away the time-slot winner against all comers.

As smooth as things were on the air, two unpublicized events brought a terrible dose of sadness to the set and would profoundly

The Lassie punch-out book was introduced in 1958 and sold well, but few mint copies still exist. The eerie Lassie punch-out figure, which looks like a Lassie fireside rug, was the only one in the book designed to be multidimensional.

affect work for the next two years. For Rudd Weatherwax these losses were a true heartbreak. They would also spell the end of the movies' most legendary dog and threaten television's best-known canine, too.

"By the time I joined the show," Jon Provost recalled, "Pal was too old to come to the set much anymore. I remember him more from the times I visited Rudd's house. He was the dog that everyone called 'the Old Man,' and it was a term of respect. As young as I was, I recognized just how much that dog meant to Rudd. Even though he was blind, deaf, and was getting stiff, Pal had the run of the house. Rudd loved that old dog as much as anyone could love an animal or a person." But although he was cared for as if he were a king, no dog, not even Pal, could live forever.

Pal was eighteen when he died in

Lassie got along with almost any kind of animal, but Jon often found himself being bitten or kicked by furry guest stars.

1958. He was years past his prime, and in his last days he was often cranky and irritable. Yet to his owner, who preferred to think of himself as Pal's friend rather than master, this dog could do no wrong. Even in extreme old age, Pal was cared for as he had been when he was a star. His place in the home and in Rudd's heart was never questioned or challenged. When Pal died, the rugged veteran dog trainer took him out on his ranch and privately buried him. Nothing was said, no words were spoken, but it was a loss that Rudd couldn't fully accept. For months he slipped in and out of a deep depression.

"He loved Pal like he loved his sons," Robert Weatherwax remembered. "It hit him very hard when he died. He buried him in a special place on the ranch and would often visit the grave."

"Dad would never again watch an MGM Lassie movie," he continued. "He just couldn't bear to see Pal. He didn't want to have to be reminded of just how much he loved that dog."

One of the things that made losing the legend a bit easier for Rudd was the amazing way that Pal's son, Lassie, Jr., responded to his trainer and to his job. This television Lassie had all his father's great majesty and presence, and he seemed to worship the ground on which Rudd walked. Like Pal, this dog would do anything for his trainer, and when put to the test he was always magnificent. Lassie, Jr., could stroll through a scene with so little effort that he often left the seasoned crew in awe. He was eager, fearless, and strong, and yet upon command he would pick up a tiny chick in his mouth and never harm it. He learned his stunts in minutes and needed very little instruction on the set. Far more than a mere dog, he was a star and he was an actor.

Spook and Jon with a dangerous friend.

Less than a year after Pal died, however, the remarkable Lassie, Jr., began to show signs of weakness, and it concerned Rudd more than he could express. Before anyone else had noticed a problem, the owner had sensed that all was not right. Lassie, Jr., wasn't as strong, his coat as glossy, or his appetite as hearty as should have been the case. Weatherwax knew that whatever was wrong with Lassie, Jr., had to be addressed and fixed. Unfortunately, as several vets would tell Rudd, the dog had to have some time off. He had a tumor and would need surgery followed by a long rest. If he lived, they said, he might never work again. The Lassie who had held the show's viewers while humans had squabbled through an entire season was very ill.

No Rest for the Weary: Finding a New Lassie

Because the TV shooting schedule was so grueling, Rudd Weatherwax worked his Lassies for only about five years before retiring them. But this rapid rate of Lassie turnover meant that he had to begin looking for a new Lassie when the current star was only in his second year of work. The dog that replaced Lassie would have to be a male between two and three years old who had been trained for at least two years.

The first step in creating a new Lassie involved securing a mate for the current star. The female needed to be a registered sable-and-white dog who carried a white factor, which meant that she had the genes to produce white puppies as well as the traditional sable-and-whites. Genetically, this type of mother was required to ensure the birth of a dog that would have enough white to match the markings of his father.

At birth the male puppies were checked to see if they had four white feet, a white blaze, and a full white collar. Many collies have four white feet, a few have a full white collar, but the thin white blaze is rare indeed. The markings had to be perfect—makeup and dyes were never used. If none matched his father, another breeding was needed. Sometimes it took hundreds of puppies to create that special Lassie look.

When a potential Lassie was found, Rudd then put him through an educational program that took him slowly from canine kindergarten through elementary and high school and eventually on to college, all to prepare him for show business. If the dog couldn't master the education it was back to the drawing board, and another breeding was set up to find another Lassie.

A Lassie puppy who had been found acceptable was then introduced to life in the public eye. He became a constant visitor to the television set and began to travel all around the country. But if the studio or the travel made him uncomfortable, the puppy was out.

"It's funny," Robert Weatherwax mused, "sometimes we could get just the right dog the first time we tried, and other times it took years and scores of litters. But Dad wouldn't be satisfied until everything came together—the Lassie look, the education, and the socialization. Only when he was satisfied that all three elements were perfect did he know he had the next Lassie." And then it would start all over again.

As a businessman Rudd should have focused his attention on training one of Lassie, Jr.'s, pups as a replacement dog. But he couldn't. With the pain caused by Pal's death, and the day-to-day fight just to get Lassie, Jr., through his battle with cancer, Rudd had very little spirit left to train another dog. Besides, he hadn't been able to find the right dog during any of his numerous breedings. Time and time again he had gotten close, but that special Lassie look—narrow blaze, full white collar, and four white feet—was just not there. The only dog he might be able to use was a good year away from being well trained enough to work on television. And even if he were ready, this dog wasn't a close enough clone to fool the show's viewers. His blaze was far too wide.

Lassie, Jr., is justifiably proud of his brood, but none of these puppies had the right markings to become the next Lassie.

The series was in no position to wait for Rudd or Lassie, Jr., however. It had to continue filming, and even though Rudd knew that he wasn't anywhere near ready, an unprepared substitute dog, one of Lassie, Jr.'s, own sons—he would be nicknamed Spook—was brought in midway through the 1959 season. His first scene called for him to enter the kitchen and walk over to June Lockhart. Everyone held their breath as the dog followed Rudd's commands and walked through the shot like a seasoned pro. But as he neared June and the end of the initial scene, a huge light positioned just above the dog's head gave way. Just before the director yelled "Cut," the light came crashing to the ground.

"The poor dog was frightened out of his mind," June remembered. "The noise, the nearness of where it had happened, the fact that it was so unexpected and his first time on the set, it panicked him. Before anyone could grab him and calm him down, he bolted from the room and out the door. He was off the set in a flash."

It took some time for Rudd and the others to find the dog, who was eventually discovered shaking behind the barn set. When he was returned to the kitchen set, he grew very apprehensive. His eyes scanned the lights and all the other paraphernalia suspended from the ceiling. His body became more tense with each step he was forced to take. And when June approached him he had to be held to keep him from running away again.

"Rudd was having to force-train this dog at the same time he also was trying to save the other dog's life," June explained. "There couldn't have been a worse way for him to have started."

The circus often came to Calverton, and Timmy always managed to get a job doing something simple and safe like feeding tigers. Here Spook seems to sense that there are better places to be than around wild animals.

Force-training meant that Rudd was attempting to bring Spook straight from kindergarten to college, teaching a dog who barely knew "Sit" or "Beg" how to show emotion and act as if it understood the nuances of human moods and speech. Normally it took years of gentle prodding and thousands of hours of patient training to teach the hundreds of commands necessary for this. Now Rudd was teaching them as needed, on the set, in front of the impatient crew, and with the clock ticking. The director needed action, and Rudd knew that the dog needed great understanding. Even under ideal circumstances it would have been the biggest challenge of Rudd's career, but given the near tragic way the collie had spent his first day on the set, the situation proved all but impossible.

The Birth of Venus it isn't, but Lassie and Timmy couldn't look more beatific in this surreal Easter tableau.

Bad girl: Lassie chomping into the Easter rabbit's face as Timmy looks on.

Rudd's job went beyond getting the new Lassie ready to do his best in front of the camera. He also had to get the dog to accept that June Lockhart, America's ideal farm mother, was not a monster. This in itself appeared to be almost an impossibility: the dog was scared to death of her. Still, the show could not be filmed without having Lassie and Ruth Martin together in a large number of the scenes; he had to learn to trust her.

Each day at lunch break, Rudd would have Spook and June eat together and then go to June's trailer for a nap. Over a period

of time Spook seemed to accept that she wasn't to blame for what had happened. After a few months he even looked forward to his noon dates with her. Still, he never really liked going into the kitchen set, and he was always petrified of loud noises.

"If you look back on the film of the shows," Robert Weatherwax pointed out, "you will notice that whenever the dog came into the room, Dad immediately had him sit or lie down. He didn't want him moving around because it was just too obvious how much the dog was scared of the kitchen set. He didn't want to be in there at all! As a matter of fact, if he wasn't sitting, he would try to slowly sneak off the set."

There is little doubt that this Lassie, the very worst who ever portrayed the character, represented Rudd's best work. The mere fact that the man could gently work with an ill-prepared, shy, fearful animal who hated loud noises and unexpected moves—and make him look so good doing all the Lassie moves—is nothing less than remarkable. From the opening credits to the close, Spook's work appeared perfect. But for all that, even Rudd couldn't hide the dog's appearance: Spook had a wide white blaze running from between his ears to the powder puff on his nose, while Pal's and Lassie, Jr.'s, had been narrow. Jack Wrather, Bob Golden, and others assured Rudd that no one would notice. They were dead wrong. While no one cared that June Lockhart and Hugh Reilly had replaced Cloris Leachman and Jon Shepodd without explanation, thousands wrote demanding to know what had happened to the "real" Lassie.

Magazines and newspapers took this new Lassie as evidence that a multitude of different dogs played the lead part. Dubious of the two previous Lassies' skills, reporters had long sniped that there must be a whole kennel of different Lassies—one to fight, one to fetch, one to pray, one to bark. Rudd had explained time and time again that there was only one Lassie and that occasional doubles were used only for distance and stunt work. This new dog seemed to make the trainer out as a liar. Still, nothing was ever officially explained—the producers and sponsor didn't want to admit that Lassie had ever gotten sick or might die, and after a while the media and the fans tired of questioning what had happened.

Despite the debilitating dog problems that arose in the late 1950s, the desire to keep the Lassie industry growing pushed the Wrathers to look for new appealing elements. During the difficult period of the changing Lassies, they happened upon a particularly felicitous addition.

About the time that Lassie, Jr., first fell ill in 1958, Andy Clyde had been a guest star on one episode. In his seventies, this spry old actor had lit up a host of B westerns and had even played one of the Keystone Kops long before many of the *Lassie* cast and crew had been born. He was the consummate professional, a scene-stealer who knew the business inside out, and he brought a wealth of talent and a lifetime of experience to the part of a neighbor named Cully Wilson. He was so good and the crew liked him so much that he was quickly signed as a regular. In times of distress, Cully's warm smile brightened up the set.

Hugh Reilly, like everyone else, became a big fan—and this in spite of the fact that Clyde's arrival meant fewer scenes for Hugh's Paul. "Andy was seventy-six years old when he was doing the show, and he could still learn the longest darn script in no time. But if he stumbled a little on a line, he would incorporate all of those blinking things that he used to do on the Keystone Kops and it made his character twice the role that it had been. They just let the cameras roll until Andy stopped talking."

With Clyde in tow and Rudd doing the best he could with the new dog, the show remained a hit, now always making the week's top twenty and sometimes pushing into the top ten. Just how

Playing the kindly neighbor Cully Wilson, Andy Clyde stole scene after scene with his comedic facial expressions and western slang.

On the Road Again

Like the traveling salesman he was, Lassie was forever on the road, helping to publicize either his movies or his TV show. But the circumstances of his travel were a lot more luxurious than those of any Fuller Brush man. In the early days of television Lassie often flew in his own plane or rode in one of Rudd's air-conditioned station wagons. On long trips when the dog flew commercially, Lassie always sat in first class with Weatherwax.

At hotels, too, Lassie received first-class treatment. Ordinarily the best places wouldn't have allowed a dog at all, but once Lassie became a star, few turned him down. Indeed most bragged about having the famous canine staying with them. One of his requirements, however, was for a room with two beds, probably so that Rudd wouldn't have to sleep on the floor at Lassie's feet.

At home Lassie ate a unique homemade stew of steak, vegetables, and garlic, with a side dish of cottage cheese. But when he traveled he relied on Dinty Moore beef stew. (Campbell's never found out about this use of a rival product.) Whenever Lassie was on the road he also drank bottled water, for no one could afford for him to pick up a germ and miss a few days of filming.

A rolling stone can get a little lonely, so wherever Lassie traveled he usually took along his own pet dog to keep him company. Although the identities of most of these dogs are now lost, for many years a small silky terrier kept Baby (Lassie III) company. And today's Lassie, Howard, is accompanied by a pet Jack Russell terrier named Melvin.

TWA was the first airline to offer Lassie special treatment, even giving him his own carry-on bag and a first-class seat.

big a hit was proved when Campbell's offered a Lassie billfold in 1959. A commercial spot, shown during the show, explained that to get your billfold—complete with a picture of Lassie on the front—all you had to do was send in five different labels from Campbell's soup cans. Besides the commercials, a special episode of *Lassie* was written including the billfold as a part of the plot. Six months later, when the food giant closed down the offer, 1,343,509 billfolds had been sent out. That meant that over 6.7 million cans of soup had been sold. Ironically, the photo on the billfold depicted not the current dog playing Lassie but Lassie, Jr., his ailing predecessor.

So great was Lassie's fame during these years that on one occasion the dog crossed network boundaries from CBS to ABC and appeared as a guest on an episode of *The Donna Reed Show*. In this often rerun episode, the Stone family visits Hollywood wanting to meet their favorite big stars. Time and time again they come close to an encounter with a famous actor or actress only to have an unforeseen problem get in their way. Finally, as they pack to return home, who should show up but Lassie—and what wholesome American family could ask for more?

Spook remained on the set until midway through the 1960/1

Campbell's offered viewers a chance to obtain their very own Lassie wallet, "made of rich brown plastic." More than one and a quarter million wrote in for the 1959 offer.

Halloween was only celebrated twice during the run of the show, but each year the cast got into the spirit anyway. In this shot Jon is dressed up as a devil, while June and Lassie look on, strangely angelic.

season, when he was summarily replaced by a beautiful and relaxed new Lassie affectionately known as Baby. (The replacement took place in mid-show: During one sequence Spook runs off to retrieve a stick but the dog who returns with it is Baby.) By the beginning of filming the 1961 season things couldn't have been better on the *Lassie* set. Rudd's intelligent new dog, an offspring of Lassie, Jr., was immediately embraced by both cast and crew, and like his father and grandfather, Lassie III loved the set and the action. For Rudd, the long months of dealing with a dog ill-suited for film work were over, and Spook was more than grateful to be home.

Jon Provost, the primary person who worked with each of the Lassies, recognized Baby's amazing abilities from the very first day of filming. It was obvious that he was remarkably well trained. "People would always ask me, how do you get Lassie to do all that stuff?" Provost remembered. "In reality, this Lassie wouldn't even listen to me. He was just tuned in to his trainers. Yet, more than just training, this dog was also real smart. Once I was up at Rudd's ranch on a visit. There was a pond about a quarter of the mile from the house, and I was down there fishing. Well, Rudd and Lassie were with me and Rudd ran out of cigarettes. He looked at Lassie and told him to go back to the house and get him some more cigarettes. Lassie went charging off. In about five or ten minutes Lassie came back with a new pack in his mouth."

Hugh Reilly agreed, but added that even the canine training genius would make a mistake from time to time that would come back to haunt him. "Rudd gave me a beautiful female collie," he related. "She was a great dog, too. Young Lassie III had never been with a female, and Rudd wanted him mated and he asked me to bring my dog over to get acquainted. The two animals romped and played and had a wonderful time. From that day on, Lassie responded to everything I did. Just because I set him up on his first

Lassie and the Lone Ranger, two of television's biggest stars and Jack Wrather's largest money-makers, got together in 1959 to promote U.S. savings bonds. An entire episode of the show was built around this theme and included an appearance by the Lone Ranger.

Thoroughly Modern Moms

While Lassie was always the dramatic center of the TV show, the character who really held the series and the family together was the mother, first Ellen Miller and then Ruth Martin. "Without a doubt it was the mother who ran the farm," June Lockhart (Ruth Martin) recalled. "Mother was the strong one. She was certainly a liberated woman who didn't take any guff off anyone."

Ellen and Ruth may not seem very modern today, but compared to most television mothers of the fifties these two farm women were way ahead of their time. Other adult female characters were generally depicted as unthinking housewives in pearls, always following their husband's orders and living their lives just for their men and their kids. But Jan Clayton played Ellen Miller much differently.

Ellen was a hardworking widow, far from glamorous, a lady struggling to make ends meet. A full business partner in the farm with Gramps, she was independent, made her own decisions, dealt with men on their level, and was both a father and mother to her son. As a single mom, Ellen also got involved in her son's life in ways that June Cleaver or Margaret Anderson would never have considered, even going to father/son outings in her late husband's place. She camped out with Jeff and his friends, she fished, she played softball, and she was even known to toss around a football. When Gramps was sick, Ellen ran the farm alone, drove the pickup, and took care of the animals. She also sang professionally on the radio, played organ at church, occasionally wore pants, and even dated. Simply enough, Ellen was years ahead of most other women on television.

June Lockhart's Ruth Martin was a remarkably adept and impressive character, too. She often ran the farm while her husband, Paul, was away, making the decisions about purchases, crops, and livestock, and she once took a job as a fire watcher in a forestry tower. She could shoot a rifle, pitch a tent, and make a camp, and she drove all over the country without a man by her side, much like any real farm woman. In addition Ruth was educated, generous to strangers, and well versed in everything from literature to music. And she didn't allow her husband to hold her back—if she wanted to do something like fight a forest fire alongside the men, she did.

Now Ellen and Ruth could tote a bale with even the best man, but of course they still baked cookies and wore high heel shoes with freshly starched dresses. And just like Donna Stone, they could survive any disaster without smudging their makeup.

*June Lockhart,
humble farm woman.*

date, he liked me so much he wouldn't wait for his cue [during a scene with Reilly]. When I would walk in the studio every morning, the dog and I would make eye contact, and he would charge across the set and run to me. I loved that—Rudd didn't."

June Lockhart, the set's joker, kept people in stitches and teased them about almost everything on the show. The producers and Campbell's were often dismayed when she admitted that she couldn't cook a lick, that the food in the Martins' kitchen all came out of cans, and that the cookies Ruth was always making were straight out of a bag labeled "Mother's Cookies." Yet the one thing she never kidded about was Rudd's mastery. "He was the reason the show worked," Lockhart insisted. "Lassie didn't act. Lassie was a dog. It was Rudd and the people who worked with him that made the dog look as though he were acting.

"When we did a scene, and Lassie was supposed to respond to one of us as we talked, Rudd and Sam Williamson would be on stepladders just out of camera view calling to the dog and showing him where to look. The directors wanted Lassie to be observing each person as he or she spoke. So, as we spoke our lines, Sam and Rudd were making all of this noise, and we got to where we didn't even notice. Of course, it could be quite unnerving for the guest stars, who weren't used to it."

Provost added, "One thing I really learned from Rudd was respect for animals. Rudd's whole process of training was different, it was a love-guided training. He respected his Lassies, just like he respected people. It set the tone for the whole set, and I will always take that with me."

Still, no matter how happy the set was, working on *Lassie* could be confining. June's and Hugh's contracts had long clauses that forbade them from acting in other vehicles that would undermine their *Lassie* image—they couldn't play anything but wholesome, all-American characters. Unlike so many others who bridled at this facet of the business, the two actors considered it their good fortune.

As the years rolled by the writing improved—by necessity. With hundreds of episodes of *Lassie* in the can, the writers were being challenged in special ways. After all, you could only do so

many elephants on a midwestern farm, and Lassie could only pull Timmy out of the water so many times a year. In order to expand the show's creativity, the writers embraced a new theme—conservation and the environment.

Going back to its beginning, *Lassie* had always been a show that used the "balance of nature" premise as a subtle part of many of its scripts. Yet with segments that now explicitly preached saving forests, lakes, watersheds, and wildlife, Lassie was becoming the first actor to embrace a role as an environmental advocate.

Lassie and Timmy helped in replanting burned-out sections of forests. They fought to save what we now know as native wetlands. Hugh spent time rotating crops and developing plowing strategies that saved soil. Wild animals were not slaughtered when they roamed onto the farm, but instead were often captured and relocated.

Lassie hits the heights, visiting the Grand Canyon for the 1961 season premiere.

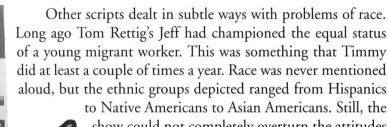

Timmy and Lassie sneakers were the rage in Calverton.

Opposite: Campbell's and CBS sent out millions of pawtographs showing Jon and Lassie III (Baby) during the early sixties. He can be distinguished from his father, Lassie, Jr., and his grandfather, Pal, by his slightly longer and thinner blaze.

Other scripts dealt in subtle ways with problems of race. Long ago Tom Rettig's Jeff had championed the equal status of a young migrant worker. This was something that Timmy did at least a couple of times a year. Race was never mentioned aloud, but the ethnic groups depicted ranged from Hispanics to Native Americans to Asian Americans. Still, the show could not completely overturn the attitudes of the times, and as Lloyd Nelson recalls, for a very long time African Americans were not written into these scripts because of Campbell's fears of a Southern boycott.

Through the use of the Cully character, the series also said a great deal about the positive contributions of aging Americans. Scripts constantly pointed out that life didn't end at forty and that wisdom was a benefit of growing old. One of Hugh Reilly's favorite scenes came during a show in which he defended Cully in front of a group of people who wanted the "crazy old animal lover"—"environmentalist" would be the modern term—put in a home.

Lassie's audience continued to grow as the years passed. By the 1962/3 season the show was earning a 41.6 percent audience share in what was supposed to be the throwaway early-Sunday-night time slot. Campbell's profits had soared some 70 percent over pre-*Lassie* days, and with the cast now included in more commercials, sales were growing even more. If there was a new product, Timmy or June introduced it, and everywhere both kids and adults were demanding more of the "real goodness" of the sponsor's soup.

Wrather Company reports indicated that by late 1961 more adults than children were watching the show. With the soup giant paying Wrather more than $7 million a year just to run commercials, the oilman's cheaply produced show was coming in like a real gusher. It was now the longest-running drama show on the air. It had become an icon. Lassie was to CBS what the dog had once been to MGM. There was so much interest in Lassie that Campbell's had veteran director Jack Hively direct two behind-the-scenes Lassie documentaries for the Wrather Company. These

From Your Friends Jon Provost "Timmy" and Lassie

© Wrather Corporation

Dog Fights

At least one out of every ten shows required Lassie to fight another member of the canine species, usually a mean wolf. It was crucial that these scenes look and sound real, but it was more important that Lassie be in no way injured during the filming.

In order to make a fight look realistic but not hurt his dogs, Rudd Weatherwax would bring in a German shepherd that was one of Lassie's favorite playmates. Lassie and the shepherd would have been kept apart for the entire week so that when they saw each other they would be excited and want to play. But first, Rudd would take the shepherd and have him made up to look menacing and more wolflike. Then a special rubber band was placed to hold up his lip where his canine teeth showed, making him appear mad; the same thing was done to Lassie, with rubber bands painted to match the dogs' coats and markings.

Sam Williamson, Rudd's assistant, would hold the shepherd and Rudd would hold Lassie, and on cue they would release the dogs and say, "Sic 'em!" The two pals were so excited to be together that they would rush across the grass at each other, roll and romp, charge at each other, and run around like mad, while all the time the cameras were rolling. Later, after the film had been processed, the sound editor would lay in the noise of an awful fight, complete with snarls, cries, yelps, and growls. On TV it looked like a real battle. Yet if viewers had just turned down the sound, they would have recognized two very happy, playful dogs.

While the fight scenes looked mean and realistic, the two dogs were only playing.

showed Lassie being trained, at home in his bedroom, sleeping on his king-sized bed, playing with his pet dog, and listening to the soothing sounds of his own hi-fi.

For Jon Provost, who couldn't seem to go anywhere without being mobbed, the whole experience was much like spending every day in an amusement park. He used the sets for playgrounds, Lassie as a playmate, and every animal that came on the set as his own private circus act.

Lloyd Nelson remembered Jon as a typical kid who just couldn't seem to get enough of animals. "It seemed that Jon worked with every domestic and wild animal known by man, and as I remember it, he was bitten by half of them. He just loved animals and he was always sticking his finger in the cages, and they'd bite him. He never learned. He was a normal everyday kid who was going to pet the kitty. The kitty might happen to be a lion, but that didn't stop Jon from treating him like a kitty."

One time Jon had to work with a chimp. On this occasion the ape's English trainer came onto the set dressed like something out of Barnum and Bailey. He wore a khaki safari suit complete with riding boots, a pith helmet, and a side arm. After filming, during which the animal was perfect, the chimp was sitting on a stool backstage, waiting for his owner to load up his gear. As Jon walked by he smiled and reached out to pat the chimp's head. In response, the animal grabbed Jon by the arm and tried to bite off his thumb. To make matters worse, the chimp started running away, dragging Jon behind with the boy's thumb still locked in his mouth. Catching up with them, the trainer pulled out his gun and fired blanks into the air at least a half dozen times before the noise caused the chimp to let go. As they hauled the ape off to a cage, Jon was rushed to the infirmary to have his thumb sewn up.

Although the ape was certainly irascible, at least it had been easy to work with on the set. Other animals, however, could be a real challenge. Many of them didn't like people or were scared of cameras, and some could be downright feisty. One time an ostrich got loose and raced the crew down Ventura Boulevard. Countless raccoons ran away and were discovered in places ranging from the

One of the best-remembered Lassie episodes involved an appearance by base-ball Hall-of-Famer Roy Campanella in 1959. In this candid shot, director Holly Morse, dialogue coach Lloyd Nelson, Campanella, and Jon Provost go over the script.

commissary to the studio's trash cans. Once when an episode was being shot in a rocky area outside Los Angeles, a kangaroo made a mad dash for freedom. The whole cast and crew chased it for miles, around rocks and up hills, but it was faster and easily escaped. Eventually it was found near a freeway some twenty miles away. Incidents like this constantly interrupted filming.

In order to enhance the family feel of the show, anytime there was an episode in which children were needed to play background parts the call went out, but not to casting directors. Instead, the cast and crew were asked to bring in their own children to play the parts of classmates, 4-H members, scouts, or church friends.

"My children all enjoyed my being on the show," Hugh Reilly recalled. "They loved Lassie and they loved getting to work on a film from time to time, too. One lovely story involved my oldest boy, David. When he was about ten, we were going to do a picture about the Little League and have as a guest star Roy Campanella, the Dodgers' great catcher. This was after Roy had been paralyzed in a car wreck. He was going to come and talk to Timmy about sportsmanship and about playing the game of baseball. They had asked David to be a part of the team to be used during the show's filming.

"On the Friday before we were to start the picture on Monday, David was playing with [actor] Stuart Whitman's kids across the street from our house, and fell out of a tree and broke his arm. I ran over, picked him up, and took him to the hospital, all the time assuring him that everything was going to be all right and that the doctors would take care of everything. Still he kept crying. Finally he said very quietly, 'Dad, I'm not crying because it hurts, I'm crying because I'm not going to get a chance to meet and work with Roy Campanella.'

"I went to Holly Morse, our chief director, and asked him what I was going to do. He said, 'You know one thing Little League always needs is a good third-base coach. You have him come, bring his glove, and wear his cast, and we'll see to it that he gets in the film.' And he did. David met Roy Campanella, and it was a wonderful thing for him." Despite the celebrity appeal of this segment, producer Bob Golden remembers that this show almost failed to air because Campbell's was nervous about casting Campanella, a black man, as a role model. Their worry was completely unfounded, for the show was a big hit everywhere, so much so that Olympian Rafer Johnson played a key role in another *Lassie* segment.

Even though so many kids appeared on the show, certain segments still had the power of real-life drama for them as they watched their parents on the screen. One particularly affecting show remains as fresh in Lockhart's mind as the week she first filmed it. It involved a car, a flat tire, a Grange meeting, and a tub full of her famous cooked ribs.

"My favorite was when I was taking the ribs to the Grange meeting," she remembered. "I took a shortcut and no one knew

"No, Lassie, this is a cheese slicer — I need a C-clamp." In one of the most memorable episodes, June Lockhart must use charades to tell Lassie what she needs to free herself from a trap.

Opposite: Timmy offers the family prayer during a publicity version of the Martins' Thanksgiving. Hugh and June never dressed this formally for the show itself.

where I was. Naturally, I had a flat tire. As I got the spare out of the trunk, it rolled away from me down the hill. When I went to get it, my foot got caught in a bear trap. At the first part of the show we had learned that there was a cougar loose in the woods. As soon as I heard the trap shut on my leg, I could hear him.

"Well, there I am, and pretty soon I hear this familiar yelp, and along comes Lassie. So I say, 'Lassie, I want you to go back to the house and get the C-clamp that is on the counter by the kitchen sink.' Of course in and around Calverton everyone left a C-clamp by the kitchen sink. Anyway, Lassie tilts his head, moans, and goes charging off toward the house. As this scene plays out in my head, I can still hear the strains of the familiar music that accompanied Lassie's running.

"Anyway, a few minutes later Lassie returns. He brings this thing back to me, I look at it and say, 'No, Lassie, this is a cheese slicer. I need the C-clamp.' Lassie cries and whimpers, so I hold up my hand in a C shape. As if the dog could understand, his eyes light up, and Lassie then goes charging off back to the house with the music in the background. Then Lassie returns with the C-clamp and I released my foot just before the cougar jumps out of the tree and eats me."

As farfetched as the plot of the show seems, one of June's kids at least found it terrifyingly affecting. "The night the show aired, my husband and I went to a party," June continued. "While we were there, I got a call from my nanny saying that my daughter Annie was beside herself and wanted to talk with me. She was so scared because I was out there in the woods with this cougar in the tree just over my head. Nothing would calm her down and let her

know that I was all right. We left the party so that I could come home and let her know that it was all show business."

In Annie and the public's minds, the new Lassie format was working well into the 1963 season. America loved the Martins and the ratings were as good as ever (the show was number thirteen by year's end), but there was a problem. Back in 1956, Bob Maxwell had been concerned when Tom Rettig grew too old to play a little boy. Seven years later, even though Jon Provost was small for a fourteen-year-old, Jack Wrather was now becoming worried about how much longer the character of Timmy would work.

With this in mind, he took the cast and crew out to more and more location shoots. In many of these he separated Timmy and Lassie from the family, while in others he removed Lassie altogether and allowed her to interact with new people. The biggest of these experiments was a five-parter shot in the High Sierras called "The Journey."

Lassie and Timmy hitch a ride in a hot-air balloon in Lassie's Great Adventure, *the first time in more than a decade that the dog did not fly first class.*

This sequence marked the first time since the MGM days that Lassie had been filmed in color. It also portrayed the biggest calamity ever to befall the dog and his young master. During these segments, the two were lost in the wilderness hundreds of miles from home, surviving only through cunning and luck. In February 1963, Americans tuned in by the millions and pushed the ratings through the roof. Ironically, Campbell's had initially fought this and all the other multipart adventures. This type of programming had not been attempted with television dramas, and they felt that the viewers might not like having to tune in for weeks to find out what had happened. But as the ratings built week after week, they found out just how wrong they were. Three of the five segments hit their week's top ten, and overall

"The Journey" was so successful that the five-parter was then hurriedly put together into movie form and released through 20th Century–Fox as *Lassie's Great Adventure*. Despite the fact that it had already aired on television, Lassie's first return to the big screen in almost fifteen years made money, too; perhaps the viewers who had seen the very picturesque shows on black-and-white televisions now wanted to see them in something other than shades of gray.

Another multiparter involved Lassie being trapped on a truck and having to find her way hundreds of miles to the Martin farm. The trip supposedly takes months, and during that time Timmy gives up hope that he will ever see his dog again. As the viewer hangs on each mile, much as in Eric Knight's original book, Lassie struggles home, and in the end the boy and dog are reunited.

In Lassie's Great Adventure, Timmy and Lassie become separated and Lassie, played by Baby, trails him to a cabin, unaware that a seven-foot-tall Indian is behind the door.

While these two *Lassie* miniseries earned great ratings and proved the durability of both the dog and Provost, the five-part segment "Disappearance" gave the dog a real chance to stand on his own. In this mini-movie Lassie swims, fights fires, and parachutes out of planes. No longer just a smart dog, now Lassie was almost Superdog. The plot picks up with the Martins leaving home for a trip. While on vacation at Lake Superior, Lassie is first lost in a flood and then nursed back to health by a ranger named Corey Stuart. Over the course of the next few weeks Lassie battles a forest fire in the Midwest and rescues the ranger in an Oregon avalanche. But finally the ranger discovers the dog's real owner and brings him back to the farm. As Stuart drives off, the dog follows for an instant, and then returns to Timmy.

The ratings for this *Lassie* adventure were again in the top ten, a fact that the soup giant and the Wrathers noted and filed away for future consideration. Provost's contract was coming up on option, and the rest of the cast's fate would be determined by what was decided to be in the best interest of the boy's role. One way or another, Jack Wrather was not going to replay the misery that had happened the last time the show had faced cast changes.

Lassie and the family pose for a special Christmas shot.

In a *TV Guide* interview the producer seemed to clear the way for Provost's departure when he suggested that *Lassie* would go on forever. "There will always be room for a boy and his dog on television. At some point we'll just have to find another little boy," he revealed. Yet behind the scenes he was planning something far different.

"I was just tired of being Timmy everywhere I went," Provost admitted when he was given the opportunity to sign up for three more years of *Lassie.* "I couldn't see myself being Timmy until I was seventeen or eighteen years old.

"You know, in all the years I worked on *Lassie*, I was in school but I was never in a particular grade. I never had a birthday, I never lost teeth—when I really did, they would put false ones in. My age was never talked about. In that sense I was in a vacuum. The character wasn't changing. If they had let him grow up a little, maybe I would have wanted to stay on. I knew that I wasn't going to sign up for another three years, and my parents were behind me all the way."

The other cast members weren't nearly as excited. They assumed that the housecleaning was as much about money as it was about the star getting older.

Where They Are Now? II

JON PROVOST: Busy raising two kids, Provost now works in real estate and does volunteer work with Canine Companions for Independence. He still travels from time to time with Robert Weatherwax and Lassie, appearing at malls, parades, and special store openings.

HUGH REILLY: After almost five decades on the stage, Reilly has finally retired. He now lives in southern California, where he, too, works with dogs. He often catches up with former producers and directors on the golf course.

JUNE LOCKHART: One of the busiest actresses anywhere, Lockhart constantly turns up as a guest star in television movies, dramas, and comedies. She is also a longtime volunteer for International Dogs for the Hearing Impaired.

"There were times when my character was oversimplified," Hugh Reilly remembers, "but the producers and writers had their focuses to attend to. First there was the dog, and then the little boy, and then there was the mother, and then, usually, came daddy. And that made good sense because the *dog* was the story, and the dog could have been the story with any cast of characters. Still, when they dropped the four of us, and I include Andy Clyde in that, they traded four advanced salaries to go for one starting salary, and that had to be a big item in their decision to get rid of the family."

Within a week of getting his pink slip, Hugh was offered a part in a new comedy show. CBS's vice president of casting wanted him to play the professor in *Gilligan's Island*. Hugh turned it down because he wasn't interested in immediately going back to work on a full-time basis. He wanted some time with his family. If the network could have delayed the show's start for three or four months, Hugh would have taken the job. A few days later he also passed up a leading role in *Days of Our Lives*. So he knew that leaving *Lassie* was not the end of the world.

Lockhart did as well. She had loved her role as "Lassie's mother," but she also knew that there was plenty of work out there. As soon as the format change was announced, her phone was ringing too. Still, she missed the show even more than she would have guessed.

"Back then I didn't realize the real power of my character," June recalled. "I didn't realize the image I had created and what it meant to so many people. Ruth was so underwritten, so what I was able to bring to it was what made it special to me. The looks, the affection, the pats on the head, the tone and inflection. I got to bring that to her character, and that was all I thought there was. I didn't know what was being received on the other side of the screen."

The transition arranged by the show's producers involved a three-part show in which the Martins decide to move to Australia and Timmy gives Lassie to Cully, but Cully then has a heart attack and passes the dog back to the ranger who had rescued her in "The Disappearance" series. To the millions of kids who watched Timmy give Lassie away, it was an all but unforgivable act. Just as Timmy walked away from his dog, so too did many kids abandon the show. Some would return in the fall to watch the dog fight forest fires, while others would never come back. Lassie without a child was something that they didn't want to consider, something they couldn't believe in or identify with.

As Jon, June, Hugh, and Andy left the set for the final time, it suddenly seemed very empty. It was the end of an era. The crew looked around and realized that the barn and kitchen wouldn't be needed anymore. Nor would the old truck, the schoolhouse, or Cully's small farm set: it could all be thrown away as easily as yesterday's trash. To many it seemed like there had been a death in the family and no one wanted the estate.

"We all knew that it was Lassie's show," Jack Hively remembers. "We had some good people that worked with him, but we all knew that the name of the show was Lassie. One time we were shooting a scene where Lassie and Jon Provost were both leaving the room at the same time. The cameraman asked who he should follow, and I told him to follow the money. He knew exactly what I was saying."

Lassie Stay Home:
Timmy and Lassie Break Up

When the Martin family left for Australia, Lassie obviously needed to stay in America if the television show wanted to keep going. And so a well-researched plot device was introduced. As it turned out, before being allowed to enter Australia, dogs had to be placed in quarantine for six months in England. Everyone knew that Timmy would never allow this to happen, so the way was cleared for the collie to stay in the United States and be given to Ranger Corey Stuart.

Of course there were other improbabilities about the plot at this point. As June Lockhart pointed out, "We were supposed to go over there so that Paul could show the Australians how to grow things. We hadn't had a successful bean crop in six seasons. What could they have possibly learned from us?"

In the final episode of the Timmy years, Lassie's young owner never says good-bye to the dog — he simply leaves him with Cully Wilson and runs off. This scene, with Timmy explaining to Lassie why he must move and leave her behind, is as close as he gets to a real farewell.

So did Jack Wrather. Lassie was the star, the big money, and the producer knew that the dog could still bring fans to the TV without the help of a little boy. Over the course of the next nine years he proved this truth time and time again. But even though he was right, he was never forgiven for abandoning the premise that Eric Knight had first established.

"The best thing about the show was Lassie," Jon Provost admitted as he looked back over the three decades since he left. "Now, at this very moment, I still wish Lassie was with me. I'd love to be able to spend time with him again. He was great!"

By now Provost, who sells real estate in California, is aware that an entire generation of baby boomers feels that same way. The dog belonged with a boy and his family, solving simple problems in simple ways. Lassie should never have left home.

Eco - Dog:

Lassie the Naturalist

" *A*ll you really need is Lassie and a camera," producer Bob Golden often said. Now, with the format changing to accommodate a more adult cast, that thought would be tested.

Back in 1961, when Jack Wrather had first begun to consider how to handle the fact that Jon Provost would eventually become too old to play Timmy, the U.S. Forest Service had approached Wrather about blending more conservation elements into each program. They wanted Lassie to become a teacher so that children would grow up aware of ways they could enhance rather than destroy nature. In the past, the Forest Service had unsuccessfully attempted to get other TV shows involved in this mission. In Wrather and Golden they had found an ally. The program's scriptwriters were put to work, and from 1961 to 1964 every five or six shows had focused on something with an environmental bent.

In 1963 Lassie the activist had been seen on Forest Service signs saying, "Please don't litter." And on television that year, the show had won its highest ratings of all time; more often than not, *Lassie* was in the top ten. Still, Wrather hadn't been completely satisfied. Viewer reports indicated that the series was no longer attracting teenagers, who found little appeal in the sweet family format. Armed with this information, Wrather had concluded that what the show needed was not a boy but a good-looking man with a lot of rugged magnetism, someone like Gary Cooper. Hopefully that would add sophistication and pick up the teens without losing any of the existing audience.

Within weeks of deciding that Lassie needed an appealing male master, Wrather had forged an even deeper alliance with the Forest Service and the Department of the Interior. In exchange he was offered the use of shooting locations from Alaska and Puerto Rico to Hawaii and Maine. If he wanted, he was told, he could even take Lassie to Congress, the Washington Monument, and the Lincoln Memorial. Wherever the show and the dog wanted to go, the red carpet would be rolled out—anything to be a part of Lassie's P.R. machine.

As Wrather looked for an actor to take the lead in this grand experiment, he focused on three rugged types, finally settling on

Previous page: The best thing about Lassie during the Ranger years may have been the locations. The dog was allowed to do everything from slide down ski slopes to jump into raging rivers. Not since the days of MGM had Lassie traveled so much, and as this exuberant shot with Jed Allan shows, the dog loved it.

Snow in California

Some of *Lassie*'s most beloved shows were those that centered on Christmas, and in the world of television, where there is Christmas there must be snow. Since the series was filmed in southern California, the cast and crew usually had to go on location to places like the Grand Canyon if they needed snow for a backdrop. But that wasn't always possible.

In order to make snow when the temperature was in the nineties, the crew spread a mild detergent shampoo over everything in sight, one gallon of shampoo to one hundred gallons of water. This formula was forced out through a fire hose with two hundred pounds of pressure. The soap-snow that resulted looked like a reasonable facsimile of the real thing, but it didn't last for long. Every half hour the set would have to be resprayed.

For the actors working in heavy coats, winter caps, and boots, it was a grueling experience. The soap was slippery and made the set smell like a laundry. But at least the humans knew what the stuff was.

Lassie's learning curve was a little different. In natural settings, which this certainly was not, the dog loved to eat snow. So during the first episode using the soap-snow, he happily gobbled some down. Bad idea; not impressed. Lassie let it be known to Rudd and all those around that he didn't like working in soap. In order to shoot his scenes, the trainer had to offer him extra treats, apparently the way to almost any male's heart.

Robert Bray and Lassie IV — Mire — face the artificial elements in the aftermath of a raging intrastudio snowstorm.

Lassie's young fans reacted to him much as teens did to Elvis or the Beatles. Here Robert Bray walks proudly beside the star as they deliver an award to Smokey the Bear.

Robert Bray. The actor had grown up on a Montana ranch, worked well with animals, and had been signed right out of the Marines by RKO because he reminded the studio brass of Gary Cooper.

With the new *Lassie* format finally ready to roll, on September 20, 1964, the last family-focused *Lassie* show was presented. Two weeks earlier a three-part farewell show had begun with the Martins deciding to move to Australia; the ratings for the last of these moved the show to the top of all CBS programming for the week. Yet rather than inspiring a new wave of Lassie mania, the Martins' departure marked the start of a long period of solid but reduced ratings. Even though it wasn't immediately apparent, Wrather's formula had been partly wrong: Teenagers were not going to stop playing their Beatles records to watch a good-looking man fight forest fires.

But with the first set of *Lassie* shows now being broadcast in more than two dozen countries under the name *Jeff's Collie*, the sun never set on the Lassie empire. Tom Rettig and Jan Clayton had now been dubbed into almost every language into which Eric Knight's original book had been translated. Wrather's market was huge worldwide, but he knew it could be better. *Jeff's Collie* was getting a bit long in the tooth, so he decided it was time to bring a new family to the foreign airwaves. The owner had six solid years of Provost, Lockhart, and Reilly in the can (the year with Cloris Leachman had simply been dismissed as a bad dream), and selling these shows around the globe could make the company money for decades. Even as he fine-tuned the new Ranger version of *Lassie* for the U.S. market, he set to work selling the new *Lassie and Timmy* series and burying *Jeff's Collie* in his company vaults. *Lassie and Timmy* proved to be an easy sell both in the United States and around the world. In global syndication the show was an even bigger hit than it had been during its American heyday. Once again Wrather looked like a genius.

Halfway through Bray's first year as the new human star, CBS approached Wrather with an offer. The network was switching to an all-color format to compete with NBC, and they wanted to

Rudd Weatherwax (far left) preparing for the next scene in a 1966 shoot with dialogue coach Lloyd Nelson, director Jack Hively, and camera assistant Walter Rankin.

Opposite: Robert Bray was supposed to bring sex appeal to Lassie.

During the Ranger years the show went on location all across the United States, from forests to beaches.

shoot *Lassie* in color. They figured that with the scenic background of the national parks, the shows would become visual mini–vacation travelogues, perfect for recruiting visitors. To persuade Wrather to make the change to color, CBS offered a two-year renewal at almost $14 million. If he had harbored any doubts about the Ranger format before, Wrather now knew that he had hit the jackpot.

The new shooting schedule, the constantly shifting locations, and the unique demands placed on the dog put Rudd at something of a disadvantage. In the old days there had been a set, a few familiar location sites, and a rhythm to the show, which had been far easier for Rudd and his dog star. Now each episode seemed to demand more and more, and Lassie III, Baby, had to carry these demands on his back. Rudd knew the dog loved to work but he wasn't going to allow anyone to take advantage of his star—not even the powerful Wrather.

"Rudd Weatherwax and I would get together every Saturday and go over the scenes that I wanted Lassie to do," director Jack Hively recounted. "Rudd would study them long and hard, figuring what it was going to take out of Lassie. Sometimes Rudd would say, 'Jack, that is a little too rough. I just can't allow this.' But rather than make us rework the whole scene, he would come up with another idea that would work just as well. It was the kind of cooperation that was typical. Working with Rudd meant that it was never a chore to make this show. I got up every morning wanting to go to work.

"During the Ranger years we were all over the States," Hively continued. "We even had Lassie slide down the rocks at Sliding Rock Park in North Carolina. I did a show

Lassie was continually pulling Ranger Corey Stuart out of trouble. Over the course of four years, the dog saved him from fires, avalanches, floods, and even a broken ski lift.

where Lassie put out a forest fire herself by digging and setting backfires, and it was unbelievable what Rudd could do with that dog. Animals are frightened of fire, but he had Lassie right in the middle of it, tossing dirt on it."

Baby was an amazing dog, as good as his father and grandfather had been. He could learn any stunt in very little time and seemed to understand the needs of each scene, even sensing which direction he needed to face in order for the camera to focus on his expression. Working with him was a breeze.

"No amount of words can begin to explain just how remarkable he was," explained Hively, who as a director probably appreciated the dog more than anyone. "One time we were shooting a picture up at Big Bear. Lassie was up on a dock, and he was supposed to run down and pick this piece of paper out of the water. The dog had to go down a gangway, jump on a couple of floats, over onto another gangway, and pick that piece of paper up out of the water and go back up to where he had been. This bit hadn't been rehearsed before we got to the location, but Rudd had it worked out in a period of not more than ten minutes. All it took was walking the dog through it once or twice. It was unbelievable." Baby's extraordinary talent was a key element to the show's continued success; many viewers tuned in just to see what Lassie would do that week.

"Another time we were shooting on location on Bell Rocks," Hively continued, "and Lassie had developed a rash and had some hair falling out. Well, the hair was falling out in such a way that it exposed that he was not a she. We couldn't shut down, the schedule was too tight. The vet assured us that the dog was fine, so we shot Lassie from just the right angles to keep our secret. Jimmy Casey, our assistant director, was positioned just under the camera to watch in case Lassie's manhood was revealed. That was his whole job on this shoot. In case he saw anything he was to yell, 'Cut!' Several times he yelled at me, 'Cut, I see it!'"

That funny story foreshadowed a far more tragic event. When Baby's skin problem continued and treatments didn't help, the vets discovered cancer. The dog was dying, and there was nothing that anyone could do. Baby was seven years old, nearly retirement age for a television dog, and his hitch with the show was almost over. This should have been a time when he could enjoy romping at the ranch, having the run of the house, and living at least another decade in blissful retirement. But all Rudd could do was give him a few months of devotion and love.

"That was a very stressful situation for Rudd, when Lassie III

Lassie in print. The canine star has appeared on nine TV Guide covers, including his first with Rin Tin Tin.

Mr. Lassie Goes to Washington

On January 31, 1968, a bill was passed by Congress and signed into law by the president that put new teeth in regulations against the pollution of water and soil. This bill was called by many "the Lassie program" because the dog was so closely associated with environmental activism. Indeed "the Environmental Dog," as he was known, had been given a citation for his efforts to alert and educate people about the issue through the plots of the TV show and with public-service spots. For the congressional record, Lassie was further honored for his work by a luncheon in the Senate Dining Room on March 19, 1968, at which time he was given a plaque recognizing his environmental record by senators Edmund Muskie and George Murphy.

Lassie the Eco-Dog finally made it to the White House in 1967, where he was greeted by beautification queen Lady Bird Johnson.

died at home," Lloyd Nelson recalled. "Rudd had just bought him a shag rug to sleep on. He wrapped the dog in that rug and buried him at the ranch. When we heard of his death, it affected the crew just as if a human cast member had died."

The production team may have been in mourning, but no one panicked as they had when Lassie, Jr., had fallen ill. Lassie IV was ready to go. Known as Mire (as in "muck and mire," the former being his brother's name), he looked like his father and had a tremendous energy in his step as well as grace in his stride. While he may not have been as good at looking into the camera with expressive eyes, Mire was just as impressive when it came to working through the scripts. The public didn't notice that there was a new Lassie, and the show didn't miss a beat.

Needless to say, the Forest Service, which now had a full-time adviser on the set, was thrilled when CBS picked the show up for another three years. Never before had one program meant so much to public awareness of environmental issues. Edward P. Cliff, chief of the Service, even wrote a letter to Robert Bray: "For sixty years our men have been building a public image through their ability, integrity, warmth, and dedication. You have managed to capture and build upon that image with more skill and enthusiasm than we could have hoped for. We are proud of the job you are doing."

To America's forest rangers and to millions of viewers, Bray was almost as trustworthy as his costar. He became an idol, inspiring thousands of children to dream of becoming rangers. As the Bray years went on, however, the camera began to focus more and more on Lassie and less and less on Robert Bray. Personal problems had left him emotionally rattled. He was nearing fifty years old, but at times he looked and seemed much older. And he was drinking far too much, which would all but do him in and eventually caused another changing of the cast guard.

"Robert Bray left *Lassie* because of alcoholism," Lloyd Nelson remembered. "It was a very tragic situation." Robert Weatherwax agreed. "Bob was a great guy. When he came on the show we all loved him. It was so sad the way he allowed alcohol to take control of him. Even before he hurt himself we had to work with that prob-

Jack De Mave and Jed Allan with Hey Hey — Lassie V — finished out the Ranger run.

lem. The reshooting and the looping he caused cost a lot of money, but nobody wanted to run him off. We all understood he had personal problems, and for years they gave him every chance to work them out." Unfortunately the veteran actor couldn't come to grips and by 1968 it was obvious that he would need to be replaced.

According to the new plot development, Ranger Corey Stuart was badly burned in a fire, necessitating the Forest Service to find a new home for Lassie. When the casting call went out for a new batch of rangers, it was decided that *Lassie* should now have two costars between whom the dog could go back and forth—not so much the animal's masters but his co-workers. Essentially Lassie had become a ranger in his own right, a character who could largely function independently.

Jack De Mave, an unknown from the East Coast, was a finalist for one of the rangers. Jed Allan, a young, good-looking, western type who would eventually gain fame in daytime soaps, was under consideration for the other part. Once again auditions came down to which actors Lassie liked best—De Mave, Allan, or about five others. On the day De Mave went before Lassie, it was evident he was one choice. The next day it was Allan's turn with another group.

"What Jed did to impress Lassie showed just how much he wanted the part," Nelson recalled. "Before the meeting that morning, he went to a dog kennel and romped around with a female collie in heat. Well, needless to say, our male Lassie was very impressed with Jed. Rudd turned to Bonita as Lassie literally climbed all over Jed and said, 'I've never seen him warm up that fast to anyone.' As you can imagine, the young actor got the part."

Finally CBS announced the new cast change, and the newspapers had a field day. The *Los Angeles Times* greeted the news of Lassie's new masters with mock shock. "Following the *Lassie* series on TV is becoming almost as heartrending an experience as keeping up with *Peyton Place*," the paper reported. Then it listed all the costars the dog had worked his way through over his first fourteen years. In conclusion, however, the feature's author, Hal Humphrey, tipped his hat to Lassie's staying power and talents. "The dog's acting ability still surpasses that of most of the bipeds seen on TV," he pointed out. "The look of mourning on Lassie's face when she hears

Lassie is a star all over the world, published in Japanese, Spanish, and, most commonly, German. In the Orient, Lassie's large and loyal fan base has created a huge market for collies.

of the seriousness of Ranger Stuart's injuries is as good a piece of histrionics as I've seen on my TV screen yet this season."

As Lassie and his new costars traveled the country shooting their shows, the press followed them from location to location. Lassie was "interviewed" in motel suites, at airports, and in taxicabs. In the parks people turned out to see the star, just as they had during the filming of the MGM movie *Son of Lassie*. Even in the Age of Aquarius, Lassie had drawing power.

"There was a time when we were up in the mountains of North Carolina," Bob Golden recalled. "A station wagon pulled up and the driver, a nicely dressed middle-aged woman, got out and walked up to me. She told me that her daughter was blind and wanted to meet Lassie.

"Lassie was resting at that

Same Time, Different Station...

very single year of its seventeen year run on CBS, *Lassie* placed first in its time slot, Sundays at 7:00 P.M. EST; in addition the series often ranked among the top twenty-five shows on television, the only records Nielsen keeps. The show's competition, listed below, had its work cut out.

Year (*rating)	ABC	NBC
1954	*You Asked for It*	*People Are Funny*
1955	*You Asked for It*	*It's a Great Life*
1956	*You Asked for It*	*Tales of the Seventy-seventh Bengal Lancers*
1957 (*24)	*You Asked for It*	*Ted Mack's Original Amateur Hour*
1958 (*22)	*You Asked for It*	*Saber of London*
1959 (*15)	*Colt .45*	*Riverboat*
1960	*Walt Disney Presents*	*Shirley Temple Theatre*
1961 (*15)	*Maverick*	*The Bullwinkle Show*
1962 (*21)	*Father Knows Best*	*Ensign O'Toole*
1963 (*13)	*(local programming)*	*The Bill Dana Show*
1964 (*17)	*(local programming)*	*Profiles in Courage*
1965	*Voyage to the Bottom of the Sea*	*Bell Telephone Hour*
1966	*Voyage to the Bottom of the Sea*	*Bell Telephone Hour*
1967	*Voyage to the Bottom of the Sea*	*(local programming)*
1968	*Land of the Giants*	*The New Adventures of Huckleberry Finn*
1969	*Land of the Giants*	*Wild Kingdom*
1970	*The Young Rebels*	*Wild Kingdom*

time, so I called over to Rudd, explained the situation, and he went to get the dog. The blind girl got out of the station wagon, her face filled with anticipation, and waited to meet Lassie. When Rudd returned, he signaled for the dog to stand beside the little girl. As he did, she wrapped her arms around his neck and whispered, 'You are just as beautiful as I knew you would be.' At that moment, I began to understand just how important Lassie was to so many people."

On another occasion Golden watched as hundreds of children from a school for the disabled in southern California waited at a large park to see the dog. They had been well behaved in the

Francesco Scavullo, celebrity and fashion photographer extraordinaire, sweet-talks the look out of Lassie.

Recipe for Success

Recipe Dog Food was introduced by Campbell's in 1969 with the endorsement of Lassie, and the brand immediately took off. That first year the company brought in more than $10 million but by the third year Campbell's was making $40 million.

Just how much did Lassie have to do with the success of Recipe? In addition to his face on the can and his active involvement as the product's spokesdog, the very recipe for Recipe was supposed to have been based on the homemade stew mixture Rudd made for Lassie. Lassie's glowing health, publicity claimed, was based on the quality of his dining experience. To help push sales, Recipe also paid Rudd to write a dog-training manual called *The Lassie Method,* which the company used as a premium offer. Like the Lassie photos, rings, and billfolds that had been given out before, these manuals were a winner for the soup giant. The dog and the book created interest, and that interest rang up a dog-food success story like few others.

hours before Lassie had shown up, but when the dog arrived and jumped out of the car, they went wild. En masse they rushed past their teachers and mobbed Rudd and the dog. It was like watching teenagers go after Elvis or the Beatles.

"One boy who visited our set just looked at the dog and sighed, 'I wish I was Lassie!' Can you imagine that?" Golden said with a chuckle. "It had gotten to the point where kids didn't just want to *own* Lassie, they wanted to *be* Lassie!"

For three years the Allan/De Mave team worked with Lassie most of the time. Occasionally the dog traveled alone, interacting with guest stars like Paul Petersen, Mike Farrell, or the young "Suzy" Sommers, as Suzanne called herself then. Lassie seemed to have a nose for young talent, and a host of Hollywood actors initiated their careers by working with the dog.

"It was a great place for them to start," Golden said, smiling. "Even if they were a rank novice, it didn't matter. All they had to do was say things like 'What is it, girl?' and then chase the dog. Jan-Michael Vincent did that for five or six episodes." So did Suzanne Cupito (a.k.a. Morgan Brittany), Victor French, Ken Osmond, and Richard Kiel. Still, no matter who was at his side, the facts were plain: Lassie continued to be the star, year after year after year.

"In 1968, when I first worked with Lassie, I was well known," recalled Paul Petersen, best known as Jeff Stone on *The Donna Reed Show*. "I had had a couple of hit records, appeared in some movies, and thought of myself as a real television star. Well, on the first day of shooting, I had to run into

A very young (indeed hardly recognizable) Suzanne Sommers appeared on Lassie in 1964, playing the role of a rancher's daughter. She is given a collie puppy, and Lassie is later obliged to rescue both of them from flood waters.

a burning barn and help Lassie rescue some animals. Rudd Weatherwax and Jack Hively called me over right before I was to do the scene. I expected them to ask me to help the dog if he got into any trouble. Instead, they informed me to 'Be careful in there. We don't want you stepping on Lassie's feet. He's too valuable to have some actor step on him!'

"A few days later we were filming a scene where Lassie and I are swimming for our lives out in this lake," Petersen continued. "It was cold, and the crew was bundled up in coats, while the dog and I were out in water that couldn't have been much more than forty degrees. It seemed to take forever for the director to give the signal to cut. When he did, three sets of arms came into the water and plucked Lassie out. In seconds they were rubbing him down with warm towels and hitting him with hot air from a hair dryer. I was still out in the water! Finally, one of the grips noticed me and gave me a hand. As I climbed out, one of the guys toweling off Lassie saw me and tossed me a towel he had used on the dog. Lassie was the star and I was the other guy. Somehow, even wet and shivering, I didn't mind—I loved that dog and I still do."

So did the home network. CBS realized that while the dog was no longer in the week's top twenty, he still won his time slot, and nothing else could really come close to his numbers. The other networks knew it, too. One year NBC simply gave the time slot back to its local stations rather than challenge the collie. When the network did come back with original programming in 1968, Lassie whitewashed the show, *The New Adventures of Huck Finn*. Admitting defeat, for the next two years the peacock network ran the

The Lassie Method is a training book that demonstrates how Rudd worked with his dogs and how anyone can train their own dog in a similar manner.

THE LASSIE METHOD
■ Raising & Training Your Dog With Patience, Firmness & Love ■

■ by Rudd Weatherwax ■
Owner & Trainer of Lassie

cheaply produced *Wild Kingdom*. Even after seventeen years, Lassie still maintained his drawing power, no matter which dog played the part or how many numbers came after his name.

"You know," Hively remembered, "after so many years of working the show, the dog would seem to get bored with the work. When that happened, Rudd always had another one waiting in the wings." When Lassie IV, Mire, grew distracted, the trainer brought in Mire's son Hey Hey. As might have been predicted, Lassie V was great, too.

In 1971 Rudd became an author again when he produced a book on dog training called *The Lassie Method*. Using photos of the Lassies coupled with easy to understand step-by-step training methods, the old man of the dog world passed along his knowledge to a new generation of dog lovers. The book was widely distributed through Recipe Dog Food as a premium.

An extremely nonplussed Hey Hey allows Weatherwax to demonstrate what he insists in The Lassie Method *is "the proper way to pick up your dog."*

After all these years and all the generations that had followed in Pal's paw prints, Rudd Weatherwax was convinced that Lassie would go on forever. He couldn't imagine television without Lassie. For that matter neither could millions of fans. Ed Sullivan was the only personality at CBS who had been around longer, and to most of the world it looked like the collie would easily outlive Ed. One image in particular embodied the Lassie tradition: In Rudd's home there was a closet with a double mirror, and occasionally Lassie V would stand in front of that mirror, his reflection going on forever. Once, when Jack Hively was visiting, Rudd pointed to the dog's infinite image and said, "Jack, I'll never run out of Lassies." What Rudd couldn't have known at that time was

On cover: Whitman · 1026 · 39¢ · multicolor on every page · paint with water · just wet a brush · *Lassie* · Authorized Edition

From dog collars to board games, Lassie has long been a big player in the consumer marketplace. One product that sold well, even with its bizarre cover, was the Lassie paint-with-water book.

that a Federal Communications Commission (FCC) ruling would mean that CBS was about to run out of room for the dog.

In an effort to encourage local affiliates to generate more community-related programming, in 1971 the FCC ordered prime time moved back to 8:00 P.M. EST on Sundays. This move killed *Lassie*'s time slot. CBS didn't feel that the show would be well received in another time period and the remainder of the network's family programming was set, so they simply canceled the series.

Finally *Lassie* had come to an end; at last the great collie would rest. Or so most people thought. But Jack Wrather had other ideas. He proceeded to put together a syndication package complete with all-new episodes and lined up 97 percent of the CBS stations for the program. Campbell's stayed on, and in most areas the show moved to an even better time slot, at 7:30 P.M. By the fall premiere, 191 markets were on line, and not just for one season but for two.

In his first year of syndication Lassie pretty much roamed the country on his own, unhindered by human costars. The next season Wrather brought *Lassie* back home to a rural setting—a ranch, to be precise, run by the Holden family. Working with Lassie were Larry Wilcox, Larry Pennell, Skip Burton, Pamelyn Ferdin, Joshua Albee, and Sherry Boucher. The Holden ranch was where the dog would remain for the show's last two years. Still, this place was not the Millers', nor the Martins', and the family's kids weren't Jeff or Timmy—the updating didn't work and the characters seemed empty. In either August or early September of 1974 (depending upon the schedules of the local stations), Lassie trotted off into the sunset for the final time, after twenty years and 592 episodes. By this point no one noticed.

"When Rudd would retire a Lassie," Jack Hively remembered, "he would treat that dog as if he were the king of England. At first the dog would love the time off and the super treatment. Then, after a little while away from the set, he'd start to miss it. The dog that had been retired would watch Rudd drive away with

© COPYRIGHT 1974 FILMATION WRATHER

After *Lassie* was finally dropped from the network airwaves, CBS created a Saturday-morning cartoon version called *Lassie's Rescue Rangers* in 1973. The show, which depicted Lassie as a superdog, earned Rudd Weatherwax's deep disdain: "That's not Lassie," he remarked, "that's trash."

the new Lassie and he would bark and bark and bark. He actually got very mad that they were going to work, and he wasn't."

Now Rudd must have felt the same way. For the first time in almost thirty years he and Lassie had no place to go, nowhere to work. The tours, the fairs, the live appearances were still there, and *Lassie* continued in syndication, mostly in the early mornings, but the day-to-day work was finished. He and the dogs were home, with a wealth of knowledge and talent, a lifetime of experience, a world of fame . . . but with no place to go.

In his two years on the air, Lassie V— Hey Hey — worked with a brand-new family, the Holdens.

"The Bark" Is Back:
Fifty Years of America's Favorite Dog

Without a daily routine or a shooting schedule for which to prepare, Rudd Weatherwax and his dogs spent the next few years in anxious retirement. Rudd was a high-energy person who simply wasn't good at doing nothing. He needed to be around people and he needed to be working. There had to be another project he and Lassie could take on. With this in mind, he placed his sixth-generation Lassie into training. Yet while he was looking ahead, he wasn't forgetting about those in the past either.

"In the years after the show folded," Jack Hively remembered, "I used to go out and see Rudd a great deal. Once, he asked me if I was working, and I informed him I was about to go to work on a show. He wanted to know if I needed any money. I told him I was fine. He then reached into an old potbellied stove and pulled out a handful of money. I didn't take it, but that was just the way he was. He wanted to take care of all those around him."

Jack Wrather was another man who hadn't given up on his property; he too felt that the old dog still had some life. So while Rudd waited at home, the producer took polls and asked thousands of people hundreds of questions. He had to find out exactly what their moods were: What were Americans really thinking about current entertainment? What did they really want? Wrather knew that family films were no longer hot at the box office—most folks now had trouble believing in God, much less in a dog. Would the public, who had just endured a decade of doubt and mistrust, spend money for a Lassie movie? The experts told him no, but Wrather bucked all the evidence and decided to try for a comeback. Now he had to convince Lassie.

Weatherwax was interested, of course, but he questioned just how serious the producer was. Would this new vehicle be one that did justice to the dog's legacy? To make this film work, the Texas oilman had to have Weatherwax, and the trainer knew it. Wrather had long ago realized that Lassie and Weatherwax were two names that were tied together even more closely than Astaire and Rogers or Burns and Allen. Crosby couldn't do a road movie without Hope, and Wrather couldn't do a Lassie show or movie without Rudd. Over a drink the two hammered out an agreement, with Rudd get-

Previous page: Lassie VI— Boy — made his debut in 1978 with several of the screen's legends in The Magic of Lassie.

176

ting the assurances he wanted that the Lassie character would remain true to Eric Knight's vision. A few days later a happy and confident Wrather let it slip to the press that Lassie would soon be back in front of the cameras.

The first element of the Lassie resurrection involved a new television series for the dog. Wrather called in a crew, hired a few unknown actors, and hurriedly put together the beginnings of a new *Lassie* television series to premiere in 1978. Over the period of a few weeks the crew filmed four episodes of Wrather's new concept. The 1978 Lassie was given a family, but the show was set in an urban environment and its plots were sprinkled with contemporary social issues. The budget for the pilot was cheap, the script uninspired, the human

actors stiff, and the action limited. About the only good thing was the dogs' work. Lassie and his canine costars were on cue and full of energy. As if to convince viewers that the dog was about to make a comeback, Wrather called his latest creation *Lassie: A New Beginning*. As was soon discovered, however, this was nothing more than *Lassie: Poorly Repackaged*. CBS and the other networks passed on a whole new series and the show was patched together as a made-for-television movie.

But Jack Wrather wasn't about to give up. Even while the television show was filming, work began on a Lassie film. To make good on his plans, Wrather budgeted $3.5 million for the film and

The magical Lassie grinning in the vineyards with Jimmy Stewart during the 1978 film.

signed some major names to help Lassie move into the seventies. James Stewart would be the biggest of Lassie's costars, followed by Mickey Rooney, Pernell Roberts, Stephanie Zimbalist, and Alice Faye; to perfect the mix he added a couple of cute kids. In addition the music would be done by Pat and Debby Boone—she had just struck gold with "You Light Up My Life"—and to cover all the retail bases a book-and-record deal was put together to go with the movie. Bonita Granville Wrather and William Beaudine, a longtime *Lassie* television hand, produced the film, which not surprisingly earned a G rating. If this had been the 1950s, it would have had all the elements to make it work. But would it fly in 1977?

In late August, after shooting but before the film's premiere, Lassie VI, the latest in the distinguished line, appeared in a variety show with the Radio City Music Hall Rockettes. He did his tricks, then he joined the dancers on the chorus line. The Radio City Music Hall shows drew thousands of children each day. Followed by the public and the press, Lassie's star rose again. Offstage he was

"I knew your great-great-great grandpa," Mickey Rooney could have told Boy, his costar in The Magic of Lassie.

Opposite: The young Rooney had often stopped by the Lassie sets to visit with Pal back in the forties.

Lassie should have been a match for any professional wrestler. After all, by the time The Magic of Lassie *was filmed, the canine had thirty-five years of experience fending off lions, bears, wolves, and badgers.*

protected by two Pinkerton detectives and stayed in a $380-a-night suite at the Plaza. In Central Park he took his daily walks off leash, and when a policeman tried to make Robert Weatherwax obey the leash laws, he failed. "This is Lassie," Robert explained. "He never wears a leash." After several calls to check on the dog's identity, Lassie was left uncollared.

For the premiere of *The Magic of Lassie* in September 1979, Wrather booked Radio City Music Hall, the very theater where *Lassie Come Home* had opened in 1943. He also used Rudd and Lassie to push the publicity drive around the picture. The dog and his master were suddenly on a press tour reminiscent of decades of Lassie press tours, Lassie doing tricks and Rudd answering dog questions.

Lassie VI, though only three years old and completely unproven in front of the camera, did a super job both onstage and in the film. He looked good, he responded well to his first big challenge, and he certainly could have had a long life as a screen star. But the big dog in the chorus line was only given one shot at movie fame. While *The Magic of Lassie* wasn't a flop, it did little more than break even. The major problem with the movie, an updated musical version of the original, set in America, seemed to be that the dog was too often upstaged by the film's music. Kids wanted the dog, the adults wanted a good adventure story, and no one seemed to care much about all the singing going on. The film called itself Lassie's "most thrilling adventure yet," but was it?

The film focuses on Lassie and her beloved family, played here by Jimmy Stewart with Stephanie Zimbalist as his grand-daughter. In a shady deal, Lassie is sold to a bad guy (Pernell

Roberts). Roberts ships Lassie across the country, but she escapes and against all odds fights her way back home, meeting such luminaries as Mickey Rooney on the way. The ending is great, with Lassie returning to her family at last, and the movie is at times fun in a strange sort of way, but it was not the Lassie that patrons had hoped to rediscover. The first ten years of the series had been far more magical.

Having missed two times in a row, first on TV and now in the movies, Wrather finally seemed to understand that Lassie was not the money-maker she had once been. Times had changed, and rather than pursue another film, he was content to make money

Long-Lived Lassies

*M*ost collies, even show dogs, usually die before their eleventh birthday. Yet, except for Lassie III (Baby), who died of cancer, all the Lassies have lived at least to the age of seventeen. Mire, the Lassie with the greatest longevity, hung in until nineteen. And Robert Weatherwax thinks he knows why.

"We spend hours with our dogs each day," he explains. "We brush them, watch their diet and behavior, we get to know them as well as we do members of our family. We therefore find health-related problems earlier than many pet owners would. This is one factor, but not the biggest one.

"The Lassies live to work. They love to go and perform. Even when we retire them, we don't quit working with them or taking them with us. We still teach them, we still let them do jobs on the television or live shows, we still take them out and let them show off. Hence, they know that they have a purpose—a reason to go on living. Many show dogs are simply kept in a kennel or yard after their show days are over. Without something to look forward to, they become like many retired people do, they give up on life. They don't really die so much of old age or disease as they do loneliness and neglect. Once a dog learns to do something, his life revolves around that. Take that away and you take away any real worth he feels. Our dogs never lose their sense of worth, and because of that I believe they live far longer. I think it is the same for people, too!"

from the real gold mine—twenty years' worth of *Lassie* shows still running all around the world.

Even without television and movies Rudd could continue to pull in a few thousand dollars for live Lassie shows at state fairs or large rodeos. People still wanted to meet the dog and introduce him to their children and grandchildren. The trainer was now pushing seventy and the traveling was not as easy as it had once been. Still, his eyes shone brightest when he was showing off his dogs. They were his real wealth, and in them he could see the reward for a lifetime of hard work.

Mire was now eighteen; Hey Hey, the last television Lassie, was eleven; and Boy—Lassie VI—was four. Each had a bedroom of his own filled with mementos of his career, a double bed, a stereo, a chest full of toys, and the run of the house. Long ago the refrigerator had been rigged with special locks to keep the clever dogs from making midnight raids, and all the cabinets and outside doors had been Lassie-proofed. They were the kings, and Rudd was their servant. As he had always said, "This place is Lassie's—he bought it."

In January 1983, Arthur Space, the man who had for so long played the television vet for both the Miller and Martin families, passed away. Space had overseen so many deathbed miracles and other Lassie calamities that he could have been considered Calverton's Ben Casey for canines. Before *Lassie,* however, he had had a long and distinguished career as a character actor. But in his obituaries it was his work on *Lassie* that led: "Lassie's vet has died."

Two months later, on March 7, Robert Bray's life ended. He had made hundreds of appearances in film and television but he never worked again after he left *Lassie.* The accounts of his death began by describing him as "Lassie's ranger."

Almost six months later, on August 29, 1983, Jan Clayton, Lassie's first television mom, died of cancer at her home. Clayton, whose previous acclaim for Broadway work had been all but forgotten, was memorialized mainly for playing Ellen Miller. In life, Jan's presence had made baby boomers feel safe and secure, and her death brought with it the recognition that *Lassie* viewers, too, were getting older.

But out of death came new life as the Nickelodeon cable network brought the old *Lassie* shows back to the airways that year. The series was instantly a winner, placing at the top of Nick's daytime ratings, and suddenly a new generation of kids learned to love Lassie as much as their parents and grandparents had. A decade later, Lassie would still be an important part of Nick's lineup.

In a very real sense the fact that the old Lassie reruns were finding a new home on cable was a last hurrah for the show's owner. Indeed, just over a year later, on November 12, 1984, Jack Wrather died. He had gone from the Texas oilfields to show business, and he had struck gold in both places. While most outside the entertainment business didn't know of his connection with

Bringing up the Lassies included sharing meals at the Weatherwax table.

Lassie—or with *The Lone Ranger* and *Sergeant Preston of the Yukon,* which he also owned—those inside Hollywood were well aware of Wrather's empire.

In the middle of the Wrather empire was a collie dog. But even as Wrather's eulogy was read, Lassie's life was changing, for Rudd Weatherwax had not been untouched by the passing of the years, either. The fact was that during the last few years of his life he developed a number of health problems typical of old age. Still, he had continued to work with his dogs and to make appearances whenever he could, although his travel was now restricted to shorter trips. But his dreams continued. He was bringing along a new puppy, Lassie VII, and he was hoping that a television series would be developed for the dog. With Wrather's death, however,

The Lassie Road Show

The most important element of Lassie's live shows was his reenactment of a scene from the previous season's TV show. One year he would act out having just eaten poison—coughing, staggering, swaying, going limp, falling forward, and eventually crumpling to his side. Another time he would act as if he had just been shot, falling to the ground, trying to get up, pawing the stage, then struggling to his feet and limping off.

Lloyd Nelson often accompanied Rudd and Lassie as the show's announcer, and the thing he most remembers was how much it meant for people to meet the dog. "They were amazed by his performance, but what meant the most was getting to pet him or pose with him for a photo. Most were simply awed by his star power."

Robert Weatherwax indicates that things haven't changed much. "In 1992 we were in Illinois and an old man waited in line to meet Lassie. When he got to where we were, he stared at Lassie for some time, then softly patted his head. I was surprised that this big old man had tears in his eyes. In a few moments, he quietly leaned down and whispered, 'Thanks,' then walked off. I don't know why Lassie had meant so much to him, but it was obvious that meeting him in person was very important."

those plans now seemed farfetched. This Lassie, his last, appeared destined to become just a pet, a thought that saddened the old man.

In February 1985, Rudd Weatherwax was hospitalized for a variety of ailments. He had recently joked to Jon Provost that he would have taken better care of himself if he had known he was going to live so long. Still, he told Jon, he had no regrets. When he passed away in his hospital bed a few days later, he was seventy-seven. On that same day, February 26, a litter of Lassie's pups were born back at home. Rudd's youngest son, Robert, who had worked by his father's side with Lassie for more than twenty years, realized that the Lassie legacy now fell to him, and as he watched the puppies he solemnly accepted it.

Two days later Tom Rettig, Jon Provost, Bonita Granville Wrather, Hugh Reilly, and a host of other crew members gathered for a short memorial at a chapel in Van Hollow Cemetery. Anne Lockhart came representing her mother, who was out on a movie shoot, hundreds of fans and friends arrived, and of course the youngest Lassie was there, too.

Tom Rettig, trainer Frank Inn (who worked with the movie dog Benji), and Lloyd Nelson reminisced about their friend and co-worker. But the best eulogy that Rudd could have received was recorded in his body of work. The movies and the television shows, the six Lassies who starred in them for more than four decades, and all those who had grown up believing in Lassie—this was memorial enough for Rudd Weatherwax.

In early summer of that year, Bonita Granville Wrather sold the Lassie rights, the golden mantle of her husband's estate, to the Southbrook Company. No public record of the amount of the sale was ever released, but press

New Lassie products such as this watch continue to be released even as older objects have become collector's items. A wide variety of Lassie memorabilia now sells for more than a hundred times its original price.

185

One of the special moments in The New Lassie — *perhaps the only one — came when June Lockhart was reunited with Jon Provost and the famous collie. In this case Lassie was played by Lassie VII, known as the Old Man.*

reports estimated that she received more than $10 million for *Lassie* and the accompanying properties. If that was the case, Southbrook got a good deal. A year and a half later, Palladium Entertainment bought *Lassie* for an undisclosed figure that was rumored to be four times the previous selling price. Much more than the previous owners, Palladium realized that they could cash in on the Lassie image, largely thanks to the fact that baby boomers who had loved Lassie now had kids, and those children were watching the show. Palladium sold off merchandise rights for everything from calendars to watches, and they also put together a deal with MCA for a new television show.

The New Lassie, which first aired in 1989, was a syndicated offering that played on independent stations on Saturday afternoons. Once again it united the dog with a family, although this time Lassie lived in the suburbs, had both a girl and a boy to look after, and dealt with more pressing social issues than he had before. Will Nipper and Wendy Cox were chosen to play the children, while Dee Wallace Stone, best known as the mother in *E.T.*, and Christopher Stone, a fine actor and Dee's husband, were cast as the parents. In something of a marketing coup, Jon Provost was added to the cast as Uncle Steve. The lineup sounded good, and MCA, which was producing it, seemed to think it would fit well with the nostalgic mood of the nation.

But even though the ratings were solid and the show

weighed in at number two in syndicated weekly kids' programming, the material needed to pull in the adults wanted by the sponsors was not there. To a great extent the problems grew from a lack of thoughtful planning in the areas of both plot and character. When *Lassie* had first been broadcast back in the fifties, the series had been organized according to an established formula—the relationships were clear and any changes were carefully worked out ahead of time. But *The New Lassie* roamed everywhere. Even in a child's mind, the series wasn't logical.

One of the first and clearest instances of the new series's confusion came a few weeks into the show when June Lockhart was brought in to play Steve's long-lost foster mom and the dog's real owner, Ruth Martin. Viewers were asked to believe that Steve had once been called Timmy. Apparently the Martins had found that

Howard in his glory: the current Lassie has shown himself to be as smart and as beautiful as his seven ancestors.

they couldn't take Timmy to Australia when they left because, the new show claimed, they had never adopted him. So rather than stay, get back Lassie from Cully, and return to the farm, they simply dropped the kid in an orphan's home and never dealt with him again. Seeing June and Jon together was great, but the explanation for their separation didn't wash. Every child who had seen *Lassie* on Nick knew that Ruth wouldn't have left Timmy behind. Besides, if they hadn't adopted him in 1958, then how had he managed to stay with them for six years as a foster child? This was so absurd that no one could hope to believe it. In addition, after the show in which Timmy and Ruth were

Lassie Speaks!

Andy Andrews is a stand-up comedian who has appeared all over the world. He has opened for the likes of Bob Hope and Kenny Rogers, and has done command performances for presidents and royalty. His Lassie bit is one of the most requested:

Lassie was my favorite show. We watched it every week, but we never could figure it out. We never could figure out how a dog would understand everything the people would say, and how the people would understand everything the dog would say.

Did you ever notice how Timmy would talk to Lassie? "Lassie, Lassie, go get Mom and Dad and tell them that I am down by the beaver pond and I am stuck under a pine tree. It is a loblolly pine tree, not the long-leaf variety. They are on the north forty, Lassie, not the south forty, but the north forty, on the red tractor. Do you understand? Now go, Lassie, go!"

And Lassie would take off. She would be getting across that field, and Ruth and Paul would see Lassie coming and automatically know, "Here comes Lassie, looks like trouble."

Lassie would get up there and they would say, "What is it, Lassie, what is it, girl?"

"Woof!" That would be all Lassie would say, but Ruth would respond in a very excited voice, "Oh my God, Paul, Timmy is down by the beaver pond stuck under a loblolly pine tree!"

How did they know? I never did figure that out. I had a collie and I could never even teach him to say "Woof," much less communicate to my parents when I was in trouble. If he knew the difference in pine trees, he never told me.

In another version of Andrews's skit, Lassie rushes in during dinner, climbs up on the table, and writes the details of Timmy's distress in the mashed potatoes. After anyone's seen a few *Lassie*s, it starts to seem like a reasonable development.

The Weatherwax/ Lassie connection continues with Robert and Lassie VIII— Howard.

reunited, Ruth disappeared and was never mentioned again.

One of the show's few special moments came when Tom Rettig made an appearance as Jeff Miller. Tom never missed a step, and his moments with the dog, Lassie VII, were as solid as ever. Still, he too quickly disappeared just like June Lockhart. In another attempt at re-creating the old nostalgia, Roddy McDowall dropped by a few times. All the while, the Lassie in *The New Lassie* stood in the background and let the people's problems dominate the action. The writers never made the dog appealing enough, the week-to-week scripts were consistently disjointed, and no one really believed in what they were doing. *The New Lassie* ran for two seasons before it disappeared.

Ironically, in 1991, just as the latest television effort ground to a close, *TV Guide* declared Lassie one of television's unsinkable stars, on the same level as Bob Hope, Barbara Walters, and Johnny Carson. That same year a reorganized Palladium sold *Lassie* to a partnership led by Broadway Video, the production company for *Saturday Night Live* as well as the owner of other television classics

such as *The Lone Ranger* and *Rudolph the Red-Nosed Reindeer*. Broadway Video recognized that Lassie was a rerun star, a television icon who was still being viewed by millions all around the world, but they also realized that the great collie was much more.

Howard and his pet Jack Russell, Melvin, wishing us all a Merry Christmas.

"Lassie is not like those other television and movie characters," Rudd once pointed out to Bob Maxwell. "Superman isn't real, neither is Buck Rogers or Mickey Mouse, but Lassie is. People can touch him, they can talk to him, they can pet him, they can feed him, and they can dream that he is their dog. And with just a little luck he might have been."

The future of the Lassie name is now in the hands of Broadway Video. A movie is in the works, and there is talk of some day bringing Lassie back to the small tube. The dog himself—Lassie VIII, a.k.a. Howard—is a happy two-year-old student at home with Rudd's son Robert and his own father, Lassie VII, the Old Man.

This noble descendant of the movies' most famous dog, Pal, may just be the most beautiful of all the Lassies. But more important, in his bloodlines are the heritage, the honor, the loyalty, and the legend that make Lassie different from all other dogs. These eight Lassies have given hundreds of millions of viewers a dog that is ever loyal, faithful, and heroic.

For fifty years Lassie has been the world's most beloved animal. For a half century he has found the best in all of us and encouraged us when no one else would. For five decades he has always come home, and it has always been to our hearts. In 1993 *TV Guide* named him "America's Favorite Pet." And what is most reassuring, he probably always will be.

Acknowledgments

A great many people have given much time and effort to make this project possible. Many of them are quoted or mentioned in the text itself, and to them I extend my deepest thanks. In addition, however, several names do not appear in the book, and to these people I would like to express my gratitude: Linda Segal and Broadway Video, Linda Weatherwax, Al Burton, Marsha Cade and Campbell's Soup Company, Michael Cader and Constance Herndon of Cader Books, Karry Chapman, Arnie Cohen, Kathy Collins, Clint Collins, Rance Collins, Evan Fogelman, Barbara Mandrell, Pat Newby, Elizabeth Wasserman . . . and, of course, Lassie.

Photography credits

All photographs in this book are courtesy of Palladium Limited Partnership with the exception of the following:

Archive Photos: pp. 46, 77, 162
Campbell's Soup: pp. 75, 92, 93 top and bottom, 102, 110 bottom, 114, 131
Rance and Clint Collins collection: pp. 40, 64, 161, 185
Globe Photos: pp. 108, 130, 167 (© Nate Cutler), 183
Photofest: front cover, pp. 104, 109, 155, 174
Lloyd Nelson: pp. 142, 157
Norman Rockwell Museum at Stockbridge, printed by permission of the Norman Rockwell Family Trust, © 1993 the Norman Rockwell Family Trust: p. 39
Linda Weatherwax: pp. 19, 20, 28-29, 156, 187, 188, 189
Turner Entertainment Co., all rights reserved: pp. 13, 31, 37, 41, 53, 63, 74; *Lassie Come Home* ©1943, pp. 27, 42, 43, 44, 178; *Son of Lassie* ©1945, pp. 1, 33, 54, 55, 57, 60; *Courage of Lassie* ©1946, pp. 49, 67, 68; *Hills of Home* ©1948, p. 65 (Rance and Clint Collins collection); *The Sun Comes Up* ©1948, pp. 69, 70; *Challenge to Lassie* ©1949, pp. 71 top (Rance and Clint Collins collection), 71 bottom; *The Painted Hills* ©1951, p. 73 (Rance and Clint Collins collection)
Beinecke Rare Book and Manuscript Library, Yale University: pp. 15, 16